Connect the Dots

How Significant Life Events Impact Your Life, Leadership Style, and Competitive Performance

Dr. Joe Currier

"Connect the Dots" is a leadership development and executive coaching methodology to improve performance in business, and by extension, personal relationships. Whether a reader is seeking to improve his/her life, or attempting to better understand how human behavior determines business behavior, this book provides a conceptual rationale and practical application for a "POWER" performance:

Passion—**O**wnership—**W**ellness—**E**xcellence—**R**elationships

Published by:

FriesenPress

Suite 300 – 852 Fort Street

Victoria, BC, Canada V8W 1H8

www.friesenpress.com

Distributed to the trade by The Ingram Book Company

DEDICATION

To Carolyn

Thank You for Teaching Me
My Life's Lesson
*It's easy to be happy
in the midst of a miracle.*

*The miracle is to be happy NOW ...
in every ordinary moment!*

ACKNOWLEDGEMENT

I want to thank Nancy Scherer-Hiler
for her insights, suggestions and editorial expertise.
Your constructive input is greatly appreciated.

A special thank you to Dr. Leslie Frankfurt
for his constant encouragement and support.
You have been my friend, mentor, and colleague.

I also want to thank the men and women
who have shared their life-stories over the years.
I admire your courage and have grown from the lessons learned
from both the joy of winning and the pain of facing disappointment
and adversity. You have blessed and inspired me.
I hope to pass on your wisdom to others on their life journeys!

FOREWARD

I have gone to great lengths to protect the privacy of my clients.

I have permission to share their stories, but changed their
names and any other identifying markers. Their stories
are accurate, but their data points are altered.

TABLE OF CONTENTS

Connect the Dots

"Connect the Dots" is not a game or puzzle book. It is a book that offers a leadership development and executive coaching methodology for improved performance in business and, by extension, in personal relationships.

A wide variety of performance experts, from those in the executive boardroom to the competitive athletic arena, emphasize the importance of a secure, consistent base from which people can strive to accomplish their ambitious goals. These specialists analyze, dissect, and expand upon individuals' aspirations that otherwise could remain out of reach or outside of their comfort zones. Management gurus also encourage aspiring competitors to take personal and professional risks without fear and to freely explore new possibilities in their lives and careers.

"Emotional Intelligence" experts Daniel Goleman and Richard Boyatzis report that many hard-bitten executives consider it absurdly indulgent and financially untenable to concern themselves with theories related to the social-emotional development of executives in a world in which bottom-line performance is the yardstick of success. Goleman and Boyatzis warn, however, "As new ways of scientifically measuring human development start to bear out these leadership theories and link them directly with performance, the so called soft-side of business begins to look not so soft after all."

This book—"Connect the Dots"—draws attention to research results and clinical observations such as these, drawing its own conclusion:

Human behavior determines business behavior.

CHAPTER 1

What, So What, Now What

If you don't know where you are going, any road will get you there.

-Lewis Carroll *Alice in Wonderland*

WHAT

⇓

SO WHAT

⇓

NOW WHAT

What Do the "Dots" Represent?

As noted in the introduction, "Connect the Dots" is not a game or puzzle book. It presents a leadership development and executive coaching methodology intended to help people better understand the behaviors of themselves and others. This process is an opportunity to improve upon business results. But, it is more than that. It can also be applied to building better family ties and closer interpersonal relationships.

The "dots" in the title represent the "What," "So What," and "Now What" of our lives:

What

The first step in "connecting the dots" is to understand the "What," the driving forces behind each human being's behavior. To do this, we need to identify the specific significant events that chronicle an individual's personal and professional experiences across the expanse of a lifetime. These important occurrences, which I refer to as "marker events" are like points on a map that define the important stops along the timeline of each person's life-journey from birth to death, their life-stories.

So What

The second-step in "connecting the dots" is to understand how an individual interprets these marker events. Whether an occurrence is perceived as ego-enhancing, satisfying, and uplifting versus ego-deflating, painful and burdensome will shape an individual's core values and beliefs, which in turn will determine the choices each of us makes as a spouse, parent, peer, manager, competitor, etc. As we will see in greater detail in later chapters, events in and of themselves do not directly cause people to behave in one way or another.

It is the "So What," emotional reactions and lessons learned, as well as behaviors modeled from individuals who play prominent roles in our marker events, that shapes an individual degree of optimism, confidence, self-esteem, and a wide variety of other personal characteristics that subsequently create habits and attitudes that determine future choices and performance outcomes.

Now What

The third step in "connecting the dots" is to recognize the fact that how a person shows up and behaves in the moment, the "Now What", in roles ranging from manager-leader to husband-parent is determined in large part by the person's recognition and interpretation of the past.

How does the "Now What" manifest itself? The emotions, beliefs, and behaviors that are embedded in and arise from marker events take us in one of two common directions:

1. Into new, positive life adventures filled with confident choices, best effort, and opportunities to celebrate victories, as well as to learn from and correct mistakes without diminishing psychological well-being with negative self-talk and "can't do" thinking, or:

2. Cause us to repeat the past in a psychodrama—a kind of reenacting of events—usually filled with destructive self-criticism and abusive, controlling and threatening language that diminish the ego and leave us with a pessimistic mindset, low self-esteem, self-doubt, and a chip on the shoulder.

Making the Connections

As both a psychologist and executive coach, I have found that the great majority of people pay little if any attention to their personal histories or life-stories. This is especially true in business environments in which many people ask, "What does my life story have to do with work?" The answer, I have found, is "A great deal!"

Those who are not mindful of their personal histories tend to pay little attention to their life-stories, but see their past as a series of unconnected events or "random dots" along a chronological timeline. They simply recognize important positive markers as opportunities to celebrate the happy memories they have experienced, while believing the negative events are best left behind. "Why dredge up painful memories from the past?" they may ask. They tend not to utilize either positive or negative recollections in the context of the valuable lessons learned that shape future choices. They do not heed the warning, "Those who do not learn from history are destined to repeat it."

I Teach What I Myself Need to Learn Most

Over some 40+ years now, my clients have often become my teachers. Through the coaching and clinical processes, I have learned that every life-story (the "What" of each individual's lifeline) creates powerful lessons learned (the "So What") that ultimately show up in a person's ongoing behaviors and cause that person to either lead, follow or hide in life ("Now What").

I've also learned that we can build a more satisfying and rewarding life and career when we discover the underlying "MAP" that guides us on our individual journeys:

MAP, a concept that I will more thoroughly explore in later chapters, is an acronym for **M**otivation-**A**nd-**P**erception, two critical forces underlying our choice of behaviors. The underlying needs that motivate and drive a person to act one way or another are important variables in understanding the behavior of self and others. And the perceptions, including evolving values and beliefs, shape personality and determine habits and behaviors. Think of this concept this way:

Why does one individual react to a challenge with the pessimism and can't-do spirit of a glass-half-empty mindset, while another with very similar genetics and family experiences responds with an optimistic can-do spirit of a glass-half-full mindset? The answer lies for the most part in the impact and personal interpretations of their personal histories, their **MAP**.

Martin Seligman, author of "Learned Optimism," stands out among a host of researchers who affirm that a wide variety of key personality traits driving human behavior are learned, not hard-wired. For example, according to the evidence, when a person insists, "It's not my nature to be confrontational," that is based on historic explanations behind the choices that lead to specific avoidance behaviors.

As a follow-up to that, questions I typically ask regarding such avoidance behaviors are:

"Are your actions paying off?"

"Do they give you the results you desire?"

If the answer to these is "no," then changes may be warranted. By connecting the dots in life and "**MAP**-ing" behavior, alternatives become possible. Alternatives can come about through the dictum:

Action follows mindset.

Why Not Follow a New MAP?

Consider the sage wisdom of Nelson Mandela, a man whose past history screams of injustices that could build a case for violent retribution. Instead, on the day of his presidential inauguration, after suffering a lifetime of racial bigotry and unimaginable pain while in prison for so-called crimes related to the color of his skin rather than poor behavior, he offered a new "MAP" for the entire nation of South Africa. He asked his countrymen to put away past beliefs facilitated by racial judgments in favor of a new, nation-building, humanitarian mindset based upon equality and justice for all.

Change feels uncomfortable at first. Why change? You might wonder, "What's at risk if I change?" While considering the energy required and/or potential threat to the ego, you might consider a second, equally powerful question, "What's at risk if I don't change?"

There is a special destiny accorded all human beings: The right to celebrate a life of one's own making. Are you living authentically? Or are you following in the futile footsteps forged in your past? In my opinion, it should not take the Preamble to the United States Constitution to guarantee our right to life, liberty and the pursuit of happiness. It simply takes personal awareness, a bit of courage, and a prescription for change, the latter described in this book.

There is no rational, rewarding reason to travel life's highway blindfolded or under the influence of old habits, unexamined beliefs or directions of others who, although perhaps well intentioned, should not be in control of someone else's life. Nor is there any need for anyone to be tainted by events that were out of their control and victimized them in earlier years.

When you connect your "life" dots and "MAP" your behavior, you can answer the question: "Do my choices serve me well personally and professionally, or do they simply reflect the past by adopting the mindset and model the behavior of my life instructors such as my parents, educators, coaches, and business managers?"

The choice is yours when you connect the dots in your life:

What ... So What ... Now What?

***

Our deepest fear is not that we are inadequate.
Our deepest fear is that
we are powerful beyond measure.
We ask ourselves: Who am I to be brilliant,
gorgeous, talented and fabulous?
Actually, who are you not to be?
Your playing small does not serve the world.
When we let our own light shine,
we unconsciously give other people
permission to do the same.

—Nelson Mandela quoting
Marianne Williamson,
Author of "A Course in Miracles"

CHAPTER 2

Common ene

Power-Performance Teams
Make
Dollars and CENTS
By making
Dollars and SENSE
⇓
COMMON SENSE!

A Business Paradox

If we look inside businesses across the country and around the world, we might recognize that most organizations struggle with an ongoing business paradox in relation to what they consider to be the key ingredient of success — fundamental business process or partnerships? They often consider one to be inconsistent with the other, a paradox.

Process or Partnerships?

In my experiences, the old-style business formula for success, shown here, is not complete:

Effort $(E) \pm$ Strategy (S) = Peak Performance (Pp)

In essence, the traditional formula implies that if you work hard and work smart, you will be successful.

Business as an institution ultimately is all about numbers. How much money did we make this year? What is the profit margin? How much has the business grown? What is our market share? The same holds true in the business of professional sports. The wins vs. the losses determine the number of people who buy tickets and wear the home team's hats and jerseys, not to mention purchase cold beverages and hot food while cheering them on. All of these numbers translate into profits.

Power Performance, extraordinary and repeatable success that goes beyond the norm, is much more of a question of how you get to the numbers than about the numbers themselves.

To better understand that process, there is another variable in the formula for Power Performance, extraordinary and repeatable success that goes beyond the norm, which relates to relationships, what I refer to as the R-Factor. This changes the original formula from:

Effort $(E) \pm$ Strategy (S) = Peak Performance (Pp)

to:

$(E + S)$ x R (Relationship Factor) = Power Performance (Pp)

The R-Factor

The R-Factor[1] as included refers to passionate relationships built on mutual trust and respect. The R-Factor involves a number of rules that, when put in place, eliminate the paradox mentioned above.

At the risk of getting my academic ass kicked, I would like you to consider what I call "Rule #1 to the Success Paradox" that addresses the question regarding the primary ingredient that produces long-term bottom-line success.

Is exceptional ongoing outcome more of a question of process, strategy, and business fundamentals? OR, is it a matter of passionate partnerships— Relationships shared by individuals who play to win?

I propose that Rule #1 to the Business Success Paradox is:

There Is No Paradox!

Except in very rare instances, repeatable peak performance is about people.

My experiences have caused me to agree with men like Jim Davis, Co-Founder and Chairman of the Board of Directors of the Allegis Group, the world's premier staffing company, a rags-to-riches epic story, who said:

> **"The spirit of the people built our organization
> and are the reason that we have been so successful."**

Mr. Davis went on to say:

> *"Our success as an organization is NOT measured by
> revenue numbers. It is measured by how our partners
> feel about the company and about each other!"*

Many times and in many ways in my professional career I have seen this to be true. Following are a few examples.

Goal vs. Outcome

My impressions are further influenced by the impassioned leadership of Stephen Bisciotti, owner of the Baltimore *Ravens*, winners of the 2001 NFL Super Bowl XXXV.

Steve had invited me to be a part of his first formal meeting with his coaching staff after having taken over as majority owner when Art Modell retired. It was a privilege to meet such icons as Head Coach Brian Billick and offensive coordinator (and former Super Bowl coach of the New York *Giants*) Jim Fassel.

---

1   The R-Factor is explained in greater detail in my book, "10 Leadership Contracts: Key Strategies To Build POWER Teams"

Steve greeted the eighteen coaches with a simple question, "What is our goal for next season?"

There was silence, accompanied by eighteen men in what I call "puppy stares". No one said a word; they just quietly stared at their new boss wondering why he would ask such an obvious question.

Steve patiently and sincerely repeated the question, "Guys, what is our goal for next season?" It was a veteran defensive line coach who answered what he considered a no-brainer question, "Our goal is to win the Super Bowl."

"That makes sense, thank you," was Steve's reply. Eyes opened wide when he caught them off guard with the declaration, "But that's NOT *my* GOAL for this season ... or any future season."

Before anyone could ask, "Hey, what's the deal," Steve continued with his mission statement:

"Winning the Super Bowl is not the goal, it's the **outcome**. My goal ... the main thing ... is to build a passionate partnership between individuals who have a strong work ethic and competitive spirit and are willing to push themselves and their partners. I'm looking for men who love this incredible game of football and will watch their partners' backs."

The coaches were leaning forward anticipating his next words when Steve explained his business success prior to purchasing the NFL franchise. He said, "In my former business life, I did not drive a team of mercenaries toward financial objectives. I hired individuals with character and competency and built a partnership among men and women who have a passion to compete to win."

I suspected that Steve had the coaches wondering if he was too good to be true. I also could see that he got the men thinking and was beginning to build a special bond between individuals who up to this point in their careers had worked for owners, but may never have been in a true partnership with an owner.

There is No Such Thing As A Businessman

I was not surprised by the vision and passion of Steve's message. I had had a few very memorable sessions with the man during my tenure as a psychological consultant to his organizations.

When Steve left the room, I attempted to build upon his message by telling the coaches of a very special conversation I had with him when he was initiating a series of new strategies in his organization years earlier, prior to his purchasing the Baltimore *Ravens*.

At the time I was trying to understand what he would consider to be effective leadership in his business initiative. I asked, him, "What would a successful businessperson look like in this model?" His reply caught me off guard. "Doc," he said, "there's no such thing as a businessman (or woman)."

Steve seemed to choose his words carefully, not wanting to be misinterpreted as disparaging. "With no disrespect intended," he said, "There are 'bean-counters'—experts—who keep their eyes on the X's and O's of a business."

He referred to accountants who compile, analyze, and interpret the numbers, and recounted a list of other specialists such as HR specialists who manage employee needs and address diversity issues, lawyers who fight the good fight in courts of law, and a whole host of other worker bees who labor to fulfill the traditional business objectives across industries.

Then I detected a bit of a smile when he prepared me for the next part of the lesson. "There are bean-counters," he repeated, "and there are psychologists …

All great business leaders are ultimately psychologists."

I was not sure what he meant until he continued with a question, "What do I do in the course of a day as president of a major corporation? Stop me when you disagree with the psychological opportunities of a leader:

✓ I have to read people and size them up.

✓ I have to build meaningful relationships.

✓ I have to figure out if a person is sincere or telling me what s/he thinks I want to hear.

✓ I have to help motivate people to work hard and remain loyal to the organization and to each other.

✓ I have to have tough conversations and yet build trust and respect with men and women who may have been taught never to openly challenge authority and speak the unspeakable.

✓ I have to let people know that I recognize and celebrate their best effort, but reward according to the final outcome of their behavior.

✓ I have to convince people to trust that I believe in them especially when they begin to doubt themselves, and that I will not abandon them when a market turns ugly and victory seems out of reach.

Steve suddenly stopped and summarized his message with something simple yet unforgettable when he told me why leaders attempt to build relationships and need to drill down to understand root causes of behavior for themselves and others.

He said: **"Human behavior determines business behavior."**

In the spirit of this conversation, backed by the most consistent current research, I want to repeat:

Rule #1 to the Business Success Paradox—the ongoing struggle between Process vs. Partnership:

There is no paradox!

There are No Organizations, Only People

And there are no organizations, only people. Men and women will remain dedicated, loyal, and driven to meet or exceed institutional objectives when leaders provide them with an inspirational vision and business milieu that feels personally inclusive and supports them in relation to their own life's missions.

Whether he knew it or not, Steve was tapping into one of the oldest dictums of human behavior:

People repeat behaviors that pay off.
And they stop doing what does not pay off.

*The R-Facto*r[2], i.e., maintaining close interpersonal relationships, pays off in both personal satisfaction and impact to the financial bottom line.

---

2   For more information, see Glossary of Terms and Text References at back.

CHAPTER 3
The Power-Performance Success Formula

Working Hard and Working Smart
Alone
Will NOT Get It Done!

The One Thing

Stephen M.R. Covey, author of "The Speed of Trust ... The One Thing That Changes Everything," concludes that there is one thing that is common to every individual, relationship, team, family, organization, nation, and economy. He adds that one thing, if removed, will destroy the most powerful government, the most successful business, the most thriving economy, the most influential leadership, the greatest friendship.

What is it?

That one thing is

TRUST

!

Trust & the R-Factor

Trust is the foundation of our relationships, a key element of the **R-Factor** that I mentioned earlier.

Sweat equity and world-class business strategies are certainly two time-honored variables to build prosperous businesses, but working hard and working smart are not enough for repeatable, extraordinary performance.

Management expert Peter Drucker offers a warning:

The overwhelming majority of all strategic initiatives

that have been done correctly ... FAIL!

Why? In my opinion it is because there is a third force, what I refer to as an R-Factor. Let's look more closely at what is the R-Factor?

There are three vital components of the R-Factor:

Relationships
Relationships
RELATIONSHIPS

The three Rs actually refer to three levels of relationships[3]:

---

3   Keith Bozeman, president of TEKsystems, inspired this model when I heard him challenge his partners to build different levels of relationships with their direct reports. He said, "True leaders strive to raise the relationship bar".

Level 1 Relationships (R1)

At this level, relationships are relatively guarded, closed, or somewhat private. In a Level 1 relationship, I am willing to share certain personal information IF asked. The key to a Level 1 relationship lies in who initiates the interaction and the "conditionality" of the relationship. It is up to the other person to reach out to me. Once initiated, I consider what to share. Level 1 discussions also tend to be more intellectual, surface, data-laden, content-level, and devoid of emotion and vulnerability-based sharing. Caution often plays a prominent role in the relationship, whereby individuals are politically correct, careful not to overstep their boundaries, and wary about operating outside their personal comfort zones. One common consideration of people who prefer more "safe" and superficial Level I relationships are the questions, "Why would I want to share personal information with a colleague? What does my life have to do with business?"

Level 2 Relationships (R2)

Relationships are *proactively* open. Individuals consider the question, "What do I want you to know about me that might earn your trust and respect?" By sharing important parts of my life-story, I give you the opportunity to take a look at the people, places and things that have helped make me the person that I am. A pathway to Level 2 Relationships is to use *feeling* words and to let people know not only where life has taken me, but also how these events have helped shape my core values and beliefs.

Level 3 Relationships (R3)

Deeper interpersonal bonds are established as a result of vulnerability-based reflections. Higher levels of mutual trust and respect are formed when individuals share important parts of their authentic self and appropriately speak the unspeakable. When I share my vulnerability, empathic bonds are formed, which causes other people to take more risks. An affiliation is formed that feels more like a "brotherhood" or "family" than merely a limited business affiliation.

Level 1 relationships are not designed to build passionate partnerships nor support a Feedback Rich Environment (FRE), an invaluable component of a power performance team.

Leaders of truly exceptional teams expect Level 2 relationships and strive for Level 3 in order to better reflect the relationship component in the Power Performance (Pp) Formula.

To restate my earlier thoughts regarding the "Power Performance Success Formula," I propose:

(E + S) x R2 or R3 = Power Performance (Pp)

Working hard plus working smart, combined with Level 2 and Level 3 relationships (R2 and R3 above) produce extraordinary, repeatable success, which includes material rewards, job opportunities, low attrition, **and** personal and professional satisfaction!

The Main Thing

Members of a power performance team never forget the "main thing" that forms passionate partnerships.

I first learned of this concept from Dr. Leslie Frankfurt, a brilliant psychologist and especially compassionate human being. Dr. Les' advice to a small group of business professionals during a team building session was quite simple:

> "In business, as in life, the main thing is to
> **know** what the main thing is."

He paused ... then continued:

> "But that's not the difficult part. The main thing
> is to **keep** the main thing the main thing."

In the military, special bonds are formed to protect lives and to bring everyone home safely—soldiers know that this is the main thing. In this very dramatic example, the main thing is also forged by a sacred promise that if I am wounded or killed, I know in my **heart** that you will never leave me behind. Soldiers keep this the main thing. The mission of soldiers, after all, is to protect and defend. But that is what they do, **not who they are.** For example, every member of the United States Marine Corps knows the main thing:

Semper Fi - Always Faithful!

"Always Faithful" to the mission and to each other. While I honor our warriors and highlight the psychological contract that unites these men and women in a unique brotherhood under circumstances in which they may be at risk of losing their lives, let me bring this concept down a notch or two to the business world.

As noted in Chapter 2, Baltimore *Ravens* owner Stephen Bisciotti brought the concept of the "main thing" to his organization when he said, "Winning the Super Bowl is not my goal. It's the outcome of my goal." The "main thing" in the Baltimore Ravens NFL franchise is the passionate partnership.

Whatever you do, regardless of the uniform you wear — from khaki fatigues, a number on a jersey, or a necktie and tailored suit—the success formula for a true power performance team contains an R-Factor ... relationships built on mutual trust and respect.

CHAPTER 4

Are You a **POWER** Performer?

**A Brief Sidebar regarding
"POWER Perfomance"**

There is a long list of words to describe extraordinary levels
of success. There are books that explore peak performance,
optimal impact, and so on. Stephen Covey uses the term "Highly
Effective People" in his book, "The Seven Habits of ...."

I refer to: **POWER"** performance.

To me, the expression is more than a bumper sticker saying on
steroids. The term is an acronym used in an attempt to "connect the
dots" between key forces to build and maintain exceptional, repeatable performance. (The acronym follows on the next page.)

While business fundamentals such as knowledge, skill, ability, and
experience are essential ingredients for success, a "power" performance
is the result of institutional, interpersonal, cultural, <u>and</u> self-forces.

"POWER" Acronym

P-o-w-e-r -performers form partnerships around:

Passion
Ownership
Wellness
Excellence
Relationships

Passionate Commitment

On a power-performance team, passion is never an option.

It is an obligation to meet or exceed expectations.

Ownership...

Act as if you have skin in the game.

The spirit of ownership is measured by a belief that this is **my** company, **my** team, **my** life, **my** opportunity to ….

It is not necessarily determined by having an actual stake in a venture (although this is an important and valid motivator).

Wellness …

Through life-work balance.

Work is a vehicle to deliver individual dreams that make our one-hundred-year journey through life a satisfying and rewarding experience for ourselves and those significant others who we attempt to serve through hard work and sacrifice. Becoming successful at the expense of our health and well-being makes no sense personally or professionally. You are the "goose that lays the golden eggs." If you are not well, peak performance is impossible; we as a team are diminished.

Excellence …

Extraordinary outcome.

Power players operate within a performance culture. Results matter! While best effort is recognized and celebrated, the reward goes to the winners … those who exceed benchmark standards!

Relationships

Based on shared values, goals and expectations.

Dr. Joe Currier

Partners celebrate best efforts **and** care enough to hold one another accountable for their performance and the impact each creates.

As noted earlier, P-O-W-E-R performers add an "R-Factor" to the traditional success formula: work hard, work smart, **and** build passionate partner-relationships based on mutual trust and respect.

Last, but not least, power performers create healthy tension by building contracts based on the principle:

"My partners are my competition and my responsibility."

A "POWER" Leader

I see the reflection of a "POWER"[4] leader in the research of Russell Eisenstat, Michael Beer and their associates.[5] Their research found that leaders of High-Commitment, High-Performance (HCHP) organizations refuse to choose between people and profits.

Let's connect the dots so far. Similar to the mindset and behaviors of Stephen Bisciotti (Human behavior determines business behavior) and his predecessor Michael Salandra, power leaders recognize that social contracts between partners (R2 and R3 relationships) create extraordinary, repeatable performance outcomes.

The former president of TEKsystems and current CEO of the Allegis Group, Mr. Salandra built his reputation in a fashion consistent with four HCHP strategies noted in the aforementioned research. These are:

- First, he earned the trust of his superiors, peers, and direct reports through his openness to the unvarnished truth.

- Second, he is deeply engaged with his people, and their exchanges are direct and personal in a manner that I refer to as "straight talk between partners."

- Third, having earned legitimacy and trust as a result of 1 and 2, Michael has been able to mobilize his people around a series of clearly focused agendas.

- Finally, while HCHP leaders like Mr. Salandra are especially strong individuals, they realize that their continued success is grounded in

---

4   For more information, see Glossary of Terms and Text References at back.

5   Harvard Business Review, July-August, 2008

their legacy to build collective leadership capabilities. He has helped initiate what we refer to as a "matrix team model" in which leadership responsibility is the opportunity of any member of a team who, regardless of rank and position, can add value to a situation.

"POWER" leaders manage the tension between the need to provide extraordinary business results and the opportunity to establish meaningful interpersonal relationships. Those relationships are necessary in helping employees to build support networks to meet or exceed both personal and institutional objectives.

Speaking of a POWER leader, I had the opportunity to observe Mr. Salandra's leadership style during two economic downturns as well as the recent Wall Street meltdown. Despite the pressures and temptations to manage short-term, feel-good, one-sided, company-centric initiatives, he never lost sight of the "main thing"

relationships—Relationships—RELATIONSHIPS

Michael continued to exceed benchmark standards and add superior value under economic downturns, under so-called VUCA[6] conditions by establishing a corporate culture that is based on social values that profoundly and positively shape the lives of his employee-partners.

While many executives view their responsibility primarily in an ""either ... or" model—based either on profitability or partnerships—"POWER" leaders never lose sight of the "main thing," like a mariner guided by the North Star. And they never take the passionate commitment and sacrifice of their people for granted.

Another example, Leif Johansson of Volvo fits the model of someone who leads a POWER team. He said, "For me, the work in the organization has a soul and values and a purpose that transcends only making money."

Still another, Ed Ludwig of Becton-Dickson recognized the underlying personal "burn" of his employees when he said, "Being a CEO is like a call to bring the organization to a better place than where you found it. You can never try hard enough. [It's like] your mom telling you, 'You can do better.' "

These three leaders, Salandra, Johansson, and Ludwig, —and others like them —never underestimate the social fabric that forms a foundation beneath their strategic initiatives.

---

6 VUCA is a term used in the United States War College to denote conditions that are Volatile, Uncertain, Complex, and Ambiguous.

Dr. Joe Currier

To repeat the bottom-line, hard-core reminder of Peter Drucker:

> "The overwhelming majority of strategic change initiatives
> that have been done correctly, FAIL!"

Why? One way to answer this question may be embedded in the "POWER" equation. The philosophy and behaviors of POWER leaders are reflected in the POWER model I present here.

I challenge you to bring it into your life and career.

How would you **and** the men and women who partner with you, including your family and children, measure your **POWER**—

Passion, **O**wnership, **W**ellness, **E**xcellence and **R**elationships?

CHAPTER 5

From Victim to Perpetrator?

*"Those who do not
learn from history
are destined to repeat it."*

Philosopher and poet George Santayana

Self-Development? Others Are With Us

Self-development is a key predictor of executive performance. Self-expression, however, which is heavily influenced by one's self-esteem and self-confidence, is usually not a solo act.

There are a lot of other people who travel life's journey with us who help to shape our choices and behaviors. Not just incidental habits and familiar mannerisms of our parents and teachers stay with us, but also deeply imprinted thoughts and feelings resulting from such significant individuals impact our lives and help to form our belief systems.

These beliefs ultimately determine our degree of optimism versus pessimism, passion to compete to win versus hide in the shadow of passive compliance, and other important character traits and leadership styles. For this reason, it is important to "connect the dots" in our personal histories.

Destined to Repeat History?

The quote, "Those who do not learn from history are destined to repeat it", is not only an echo of familiar historic footsteps that herald the coming of war and a myriad of painful events against humankind. It is more commonly the self-defeating destiny of good people with good intentions who miss important opportunities to celebrate life and fail to reach their full potential. Why? The reason is because these individuals model the negative, self-defeating thinking and actions of people in their families, schools, business organizations, and teams of every kind.

You might think that all of us would learn from the mistakes of the others in our past and avoid, or at least improve upon, the self-defeating habits we observe and experience. But sadly, more typically, this is not the case. In fact, not only do many people fail to grow from the mistakes of others, they often adopt the attitudes and assumptions and thus produce more of the behavior that got them into emotional ruts and lowered their performance and self-esteem in the first place.

From Victim to Perpetrator?

One reason that people repeat the painful past is that they learn primary roles—parent, leader, partner—from those who precede them. Individuals who believe that they have been victimized by someone in authority often make a silent promise, "I will never treat anyone like that", referring to the abuse of a person in authority who wields power under the guise of, "I'm just trying to help you to succeed" or "I'm doing this for your own good." But, a promise made is not a promise kept.

Along with many of the good habits that we adopt, more often than not we model the destructive attitudes and behaviors of our parents, teachers, coaches and managers. It is not uncommon to go from victim to perpetrator by magnifying the learned attitudes and behaviors, making them go from bad to worse. An example of destructive "passing-bad-habits-forward behavior" is when someone internalizes the harsh "voice" of a parent, eclipsing the parent's curt tones. Without thinking, words come pouring out of the mouth as if possessed by the evil spirit of an out-of-control elder, often with the best of intentions.

> "I'm only trying to teach him good table manners," exhorts the exasperated parent having slapped a child who accidentally spills a glass of milk after several warnings to be more careful, mimicking his or her own parent.

> "Are you stupid? We've talked about this before; what's wrong with you?" the frustrated boss asks, leveling the questions with an even greater look of disgust than when his father intimidated him when he made a homework error.

While the parent's goal was to instruct and the boss' intention was to achieve the immediate goal of improving productivity, the outcome of both run the risk of a long-term negative impact of lowering the child or employee's confidence and self-esteem. In the case of the boss, it also inadvertently reduces loyalty to the team and the institution as a whole.

What ... So What ... Now What

WHAT. One of the secrets of effective leadership and better control over one's own life is to recognize the fact that our current behavior is shaped by the significant events of the past—what I refer to as "marker events". But these future life-shaping events are only part of the message. As mentioned earlier, there are two other questions beyond "what" happened in our lives that make us who we are today, namely "so what" and "now what"!

SO WHAT. Embedded in life-stories are emotions and beliefs that determine our degree of optimism vs. pessimism, level of risk-taking, parenting and business management styles, and other characteristics that take individuals in one of two common directions:

1. Toward the "Can Do" thinking of new, challenging life-adventures filled with confident choices outside of our comfort zones. In this case, we don't stress out over the multitude of possible negative future outcomes of our behavior, but instead strive for best effort in the face of adversity. We also look for opportunities to celebrate victories as well as to learn from mistakes without diminishing our psychological well-being with negative self-talk, like calling yourself a "dummy" and really believing it when you make a mistake. When interpersonal problems arise, we use constructive, win-win partnership strategies and attentive listening in the spirit of Stephen Covey's fifth habit ("The Seven Habits of Highly Effective People"):

"Seek first to understand, then be understood."

2. Toward "Can't Do" thinking that causes us to repeat the past in a personal psychodrama (a recurring cycle of inner tension and interpersonal conflict) that echoes the destructive behavior and abusive language from the past that diminish the ego and leave us with an emotional chip on our shoulders.

It is important to "Connect the Dots" of our "lifeline" in order to recognize how significant events (and the people in these events) impact us.

What attitudes and behaviors occur as a result of our marker events? Do these thoughts and feelings help to achieve our goals? Are we better off as a result of the lessons learned from both positive and negative life-events? Or are we diminished personally and/or professionally by the negative "takeaways" that we believe are true, when in fact they are emotional conclusions based on selective disappointing personal experiences or the inaccurate teachings and modeling of others?

NOW WHAT. All of us have important life stories. Our "lifelines"—the significant chronological events and the people in these events—impact the choices we make in the moment and help shape who we are now and who we are becoming.

How we show up today and tomorrow in the various roles we play, to a large degree, is determined by our lifelines and the lessons learned—both positive and negative—from past events. By connecting the dots, we can better control our destinies and write new self-enhancing chapters in our lives and careers.

Circular Cycles

Under ideal conditions, the **"What ... So What ... Now What"** process would move in a relatively straight line:

| Marker Events | Lessons Learned | Perception-Beliefs that shape attitudes, habits and behavior | Future Choice |

Unfortunately, that is not always the case. As I've emphasized throughout this book, most of us, at one time or another, become trapped in recurring, self-defeating cycles of behaviors. We often do not learn from the mistakes perpetrated on us by adults who are out of control. For example, you might imagine that a person would not abuse alcohol after being raised in a home traumatized by an alcoholic parent. The evidence consistently disputes this reasonable conclusion. Choices are often not made on rational options. Instead, they may be driven by distorted beliefs, hopes, and destructive models of behavior.

We often go round and round in a repetitive behavioral cycle of our own making. Or worse, we often unthinkingly model the attitudes, habits, and behaviors of others. Both are not acceptable if we hope to build a "POWER*" performance (see Chapter 4), which includes both results and satisfaction.

The trick is to break free and go off in new personal and professional directions. Sometimes change comes with a dramatic marker event that shouts, "Wake up! I'm sick and tired of feeling sick and tired!" Other times it comes with a quiet resolve:

> *"One day I finally knew what to do, and began ... "*
> -Mary Oliver

NEW SELF-ENHANCING LIFE ADVENTURES

CHAPTER 6

Climbing the Hierarchy of Human Needs

*"Destiny may lead us to a certain path ...
the rest is up to us."*

from the movie "Mrs. Palfrey at the Claremont"

The Road of Life

People constantly face choices that will take them in one direction or another in their lives and careers. The decisions they make, to a significant degree, are determined by lessons learned from previous events.

These lessons learned are **either** self-enhancing, i.e., felt right and helped build confidence, a healthy identity and independent spirit to follow one's destiny, **or**, self-defeating, i.e., when life events created negative impacts, stifled assertiveness and lowered risk-taking initiatives.

The self-enhancing lessons learned encourage us to explore new life-directions in the spirit of the well-known Army slogan, "Be all that you can be." The self-defeating beliefs that arise from painful marker events* cause us to hesitate to assert our freedom to choose. Instead, we model the behaviors of figures from our past or avoid opportunities that we deem too risky or personally out of reach.

While people are often unaware of why they either boldly move forward in life or instead hide in the shadows of upsetting marker events, the "road of life" is always the result of choices. The question is, does the individual "connect the dots" between historic marker events and the current choices faced in the moment?

Climbing the Hierarchy of Human Needs

Psychologist Abraham Maslow[7] refers to what drives individual behavior as the Hierarchy of Human Needs (Figure 3). Since marker event memories are embedded in our underlying motivation, significant historic events will *either* distort, delay or interfere with a person's underlying needs—thereby creating missed opportunities and destructive, self-defeating detours—*or* accelerate and celebrate a person's life-journey with new adventures and rewarding initiatives by satisfying healthy needs through constructive lessons learned. In the former, we tend to model the negative behavior of others, while in the latter we adopt positive attitudes and actions that redirect the negative behaviors of our parents and other life-teachers.

Whether we are aware of it or not, personal needs determine the paths we choose in our lives and careers.

Level I & II

---

7   For more information, see Glossary of Terms and Text References at back.

Levels I and II in the Hierarchy of Human Needs relate to how early deprivations may be difficult to overcome. Later in life, no matter what a person achieves, powerful marker events may continue to drag that individual back into the shadow of unsafe or needy historic memories. *Being* successful does not mean that the individual *feels* successful. Things like wealth, material rewards, power, and control may provide only temporary illusions of safety.

V. SELF-ACTUALIZATION

Experience purpose, meaning, inner potential, and express individuality

IV. PSYCHOLOGICAL

Need to be a unique individual with self-esteem and to be accepted by others: compete, achieve, gain recognition

III. SOCIAL

Need to belong, to give and receive love, appreciation, build meaningful relationships: family, friendship, intimacy

II. SAFETY

Basic need for security in a family, work environment and a social milieu that protects against hunger and violence

I. PHYSIOLOGICAL

The need for homeostasis, food, water, sleep, warmth, shelter, and clothing

Figure 3: Maslow's Hierarchy of Human Needs

When times are good, the individual relies on an old self-protective dictum: "Never get too comfortable; wait for the other shoe to drop".

Jerry Jones, the billionaire owner of the Dallas Cowboys NFL franchise, might fit the description of an individual who does not *feel* successful despite *being* successful by every definition of wealth and success. When he was interviewed on the television show "60 Minutes," Mr. Jones said that he lives in the shadow of poverty.

If we "connect the dots" in his life, it seems that while Mr. Jones currently lives and works with the prosperity and security of Dallas society at his back, it seems that marker events from his impoverished childhood drag him back to how that felt. Little seven year-old Jerry would don his white shirt and bow tie to draw customers into his father's modest grocery store. Some historic parts of Jerry still struggle to survive in the memories of standing outside of that store in Little Rock, Arkansas.

People who manage to satisfy their basic human needs for nurturance and safety (Levels I and II) have the opportunity to experience Level III (Social) and Level IV (Psychological) needs. These steps toward interpersonal and intra-personal satisfaction have both positive and negative possibilities—a fork in the road of life.

Level III & IV

Men and women who strive for Social Affiliation in a healthy, positive manner (mutually-rewarding, ego-enhancing Level III) demonstrate very different attitudes and behaviors than those who struggle with Social Dependency (negative, self-defeating Level III for self or others).

Social Affiliation --Healthy Relationships	Social Dependency Dependent--People Pleasing
Positive Level III:	Negative Level III:
Individuals who seek healthy **AFFILIATION** have a need to earn recognition and approval for their best effort and achievement WITHOUT losing their individuality, freedom, and personal authenticity.	Socially **DEPENDENT**, negative Level III individuals NEED approval and operate in the "shadows" of fear, caution, and compliance. They constantly struggle for recognition from someone they value. These individuals are habitually intimidated by their personal choices because they have an *"external locus-of-control,"* which means that they feel okay **as long as someone else says that they are okay.**

For individuals struggling with negative Level III needs, safety, satisfaction, and esteem are rarely assimilated into the self because these primary needs are not **perceived** to be within their control. These individuals often resort to behaviors that cause them to be described as "people-pleasers."

There are also multiple routes through Level IV—ego development. Individuals who take the psychological "high road" strive for recognition and acceptance, but never at the expense of the self.

The self-defeating mindset of a negative Level IV experience often bounces between a zero error tolerance (mistakes are never allowed) and an unforgiving perfectionist dilemma: "No matter how well I do, it's never good enough."

You and I are free to shape our lives and are able to fulfill our true potential when we stop living in the shadow of negative marker events. It is not a lack of ability to act that holds us back. It is the real or imagined consequences for the choices we face that cause us to hesitate. We might fear that people will be upset with us or withhold their love and approval.

Level V Behaviors and Attitudes

Maslow provides a unique label to describe individuals who rise to Level V: "Self Actualized." These individuals strive for self-expression. The U.S. Army slogan appealing for new recruits, "Be All That You Can Be," is equivalent conceptually to Maslow's Level V model.

Self-actualized individuals find fulfillment in doing the best they can do without becoming trapped in unhealthy competition with others. Self-actualized individuals do not seek fame and glory to prove that they are worthy of being loved. Nor do they seek the love and approval of everyone. Instead, they find peace and contentment in the personal satisfaction that comes with being the best that they can be with as many people as is reasonably possible.

My personal and professional experiences are consistent with Maslow's thesis. With dedicated effort, regardless of the pain and disappointment of negative marker events in their lives and the powerful hold others may have had over them, individuals can reach and maintain lives on the higher rungs of the needs hierarchy.

Relatively few individuals reach and maintain a Level V state of self-actualization. Let's connect the dots to understand why this is so. The reason is that many of us get stuck in the past, trapped in the **What** of our lives (early marker events) producing a negative **So What** (self-defeating emotions, attitudes, habits and beliefs) and, in turn, contaminate the **Now What** (by living inauthentic lives based on fear, caution and compliance, rather than pride, passion and a drive for excellence).

Meanwhile, those who successfully climb the Hierarchy of Human Needs, experience better health, well-being, fulfilling relationships and levels of achievement. They also live longer.

The exciting news?
The choice is yours!
How do you choose to live?

CHAPTER 7

How to "MAP" Human Behavior

"What gets us in trouble
is not what we know.
It's what we know
that just ain't so."

—*former Vice President Al Gore, Jr.*

"MAP" Human Behavior

Before we go on a trip, it makes sense to take a map along, even a GPS unit, to avoid wrong turns, making the journey more satisfying and productive. So wouldn't it also make sense to map our life journeys? What would it take to better manage the ride of life?

As described earlier in Chapter 1, when it comes to human behavior, MAP stands for the **M**otivation **A**nd **P**erception that helps determine our choices and directs our actions. Every human action has an underlying **M**otivation, drive or "burn." **A**nd behind a person's motivation is a series of **P**erceptions—beliefs, assumptions, judgments, etc. that, to a large extent, arise from earlier life experiences.

A person's Motivation And Perception (or "burn" and "belief") are so interconnected that it's often difficult to tell which comes first.

Every action is grounded in a desire, a **M**otivation, **A**nd influenced by the impact and outcome of previous events and the people in them: beliefs and assumptions, **P**erception.

Motivations: Can and Cannot Do

Some of our motivations are inconsequential, such as when we are motivated to stop our nose from itching so we scratch it. Others are significant. These motivations become systemic, teaching us what we can and can't do. These are not facts, but instead conclusions that we draw as the result of painful lesson learned or behavior modeled earlier in life.

"I can't speak in public," is a self-perceived, can't do behavior for many people who struggle with self esteem issues. The result is an avoidance behavior—not accepting speaking opportunities—which is motivated by Level III (Social-Interpersonal) and Level IV (Psychological-Intrapersonal) needs, such as the need to avoid social embarrassment or the belief that people will think I'm stupid and thus criticize or ostracize me.

Telling a friend, "Don't be frightened. You're very smart and know your subject," usually will not alter the avoidance behavior. This is because if we "Connect the Dots" in this lifeline, the fear of public speaking will not be anchored in the actual details of the current event or the mechanics of public speaking. It will have its roots in beliefs or **P**erceptions related to self-concept. The old quip illustrates this faulty assumptive thinking, "If you remain quiet, people might *think* you're dumb, but if you open your mouth, they'll *know* it!"

By mapping (MAP-ing) our behavior, we can better understand the situations we face and constructively consider our personal and professional strengths and weaknesses. By understanding the driving forces (motivation) and the core beliefs (perceptions that arise from marker events) behind our actions, we have the necessary information to decide whether we are on the correct path and our actions serve us well, *or* whether we are on the wrong path and we would be better served by choosing alternative behaviors.

Defective Model for Change

Most people fail in their attempts to change their negative responses to challenging situations. This is true not because they don't want to alter their behavior, nor because they refuse to work hard on an alternative strategy. The reason they fail is because they are using a defective model for change.

The model used to explain how events impact people is as follows:

Event   Emotion   Behavior

Figure 4: Model A

According to the above Model A, an event triggers a person's feelings, which in turn causes the individual to react. Consider the example of Dominick (not his real name, see Foreword). Dominick is driving home from work at a moderate rate of highway speed. He's feeling good after a successful day in the office. Out of nowhere, another driver cuts him off, forcing his way into Dominick's driving lane. Instantly, Dominick's mood changes. He becomes angry. The incident triggers road rage. According to Model A, the event—reckless maneuvering by an aggressive driver—causes Dominick to feel angry, which, in this case, triggers reactive road rage.

If a friend or a manager were coaching Dominick, she might urge him to react differently. "Don't let aggressive drivers upset you," she'd say. "Instead of letting that driver make you angry, back off and turn on a favorite radio channel to distract yourself." These are thoughtful suggestions, but will they work? Over the long run, usually not.

Hot reactions such as road rage tend to be deeply ingrained. After a wake-up call in the form of a ticket from the police or the comforting advice of a friend, the reaction may be at bay for a while, but often resurface. In this instance, in time, Dominick's change in behavior evaporates and he resorts to his old behavior. The reason why negative behavior tends to repeat itself is in the model itself. Model A proposes that an event triggers a person's emotions, which in turn shapes that behavior. But this is simply not true.

Effective Model for Change

In the effective model for change, Model B, there is an additional step embedded in between an event and a person's emotional reaction, i.e., the individual's beliefs related to the event. A person's perception and assumptions trigger the emotions, not the event itself. An individual's beliefs act like a filter, altering the person's perception.

Figure 5: Model B

If people change their underlying interpretation of an event, they will alter their emotions, which, in turn, will produce a more constructive response or reaction to the event. In this instance, when Dominick had a brush with the law for reckless endangerment with a motor vehicle, he saw himself as a victim, not a perpetrator. He complained that the police unjustly ticketed him for his reaction. During an executive coaching session he adamantly protested, "I was just minding my business. That idiot cut me off. It was not my fault. He made me angry!"

The short version of this story is that Dominick believed that the other driver was trying to take advantage of him. "Who the heck does he think he's pushing around?" he asked. "Does he think that I'll just roll over like some kind of wimp?" Dominick decided, as usual, to fight back. Dominick had the reputation of a "hot reactor"—a man with a short emotional fuse.

"MAP"-ing Behavior

Let's MAP Dominick's behavior. These reactive emotions were common for Dominick. He was used to feeling pushed around and abused. Dominick's life had been filled with a recurring theme resulting from early marker events that took place between him and his father, recurring events that shaped his perception of the world.

As a child and teenager, his Dad—a good man, who thought he was helping his son—constantly criticized him, as his own father had done to him. Dominick's father thought he was challenging his son to improve his attention to schoolwork when he would say, "You're an idiot," whenever Dominick made a mistake. Also, during his elementary and middle school years, other kids picked on him for being overweight. Without admitting it to himself, Dominick began to feel like a loser.

Connect the Dots

Motivation	And	Perception
On the surface, Dominick appears to be a passionate small business owner who is always in a hurry. When he crosses the line between passion and abuse, it is always with a good excuse. Dominick has a victim-mentality with a mantra, "I was minding my business, when he cut me off …" (Negative Level III, IV needs.)	**WHAT** Significant Life Events * **SO WHAT** Lessons Learned * **NOW WHAT** How I show up in the current event	Dominick feels stupid. The chip on his shoulder is an historic reminder that he will never measure up to his father's expectations. He is a man on a mission: **"You can't push me around. I'm no dope."** His business success is his way of seeking his Dad's attention and respect.

Figure 6.

Dominick is a blue-collar entrepreneur, who struggles to manage his anger. He was polite and patient when we explored his perceptions of the highway incident. I believe that he initially thought my inquiry was little more than psycho-babble. He gradually changed his mind when asked to consider a different scenario.

We went through the incident step by step … to connect the dots. "You're driving home at a safe, reasonable speed, minding your own business. Suddenly you're ambushed by a reckless driver."

I asked Dominick how he felt at this point. He described his anger in rather graphic street language.

Then I added one further piece of information. "This driver is not an aggressive road warrior. He is a frantic father rushing his five-month-old child to a hospital emergency room. The baby has a raging fever and is struggling to breathe."

I sensed an immediate change in Dominick's emotions. The anger in his face shifted to one of compassion. When asked how he might react in this situation, he quickly responded that he would give way–"I'd move aside. I only wish that I was a cop so I could part the traffic like Moses parted the Red Sea."

What changed? The event is still the same—an aggressive driver cuts Dominick off. Why are his emotions different? Dominick has an alternative, less ego-threatening interpretation of the event now.

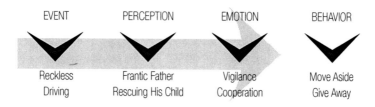

EVENT	PERCEPTION	EMOTION	BEHAVIOR
Reckless Driving	Frantic Father Rescuing His Child	Vigilance Cooperation	Move Aside Give Away

Figure 7

Whether a person knowingly or unintentionally creates a problem for us, the effective response is to avoid destructive, self-defeating confrontation. Remember what your Mom taught you: "If you're not part of the solution, you're part of the problem!"

CHAPTER 8
Thinking Out Loud

Question:
Do you choose to suffer

Or

Do you live authentically

?How's Dominick[8] Doing?

"... and he lived happily ever after."

"... and he lived happily ever after." That's how fairy tales usually end. I'd like to tell you that that is how Dominick's story ends too. If so, it would go like this: Dominick learned to manage his anger, changed his reactive behaviors, went on to live the values that served him and his family, and built a successful, satisfying career!

I would *like* to tell you that, but that is not what actually happened. Dominick did very well for nearly six months following psychotherapy. His panic attacks disappeared and he struggled to change his outlook on life in general and his aggressive "hot buttons" in particular. The reactive behaviors temporarily changed, but his mindset did not. Underneath it all, it was as if he was rehearsing for the victim role that Robert DeNiro brought to life in the movie, "Taxi Driver", always ready to ask, "Are you talking to me?!"

Dominick eventually reverted back to his old habits. His road rage behavior reappeared and the chip on his shoulder grew nearly as big as his bruised ego. Dominick took more and more of his anger home, which eventually overpowered the love in his marriage.

The last time I saw Dominick he told me that his passion cost him his marriage, but built a successful business. He did not like it when I asked him, "How's that working for you?" "Are you mocking me?" he barked. "No," I replied. "It seems to me that you're choosing to suffer rather than to live authentically." The hot-reactive look in his eyes softened slightly when I assured him that I did not intend to trivialize, judge, or certainly mock him. In fact, I identified with his struggle to change a cycle of behavior that was obviously not working.

Identifying with Dominick

I told Dominick that I myself had been asked that very question, "How's that working for you?," years ago by Mary Goldenson, during a workshop she was leading on exploring the self . At that time, I was struggling with a self-defeating set of behaviors of my own. I recall saying to Mary, "You'd think that I'd know better." I was raised by a wonderful mother, who devoted her life to raising three sons as a single parent. But as wonderful as she was, my mother had a habit that drove me up a wall. Whenever my brothers or I would

---

8   Dominick was referred because he experienced a series of panic attacks, which he misdiagnosed as heart attacks. Instead of initiating a stress management process, he rushed himself to an Emergency Room, where he was treated and released with the advice, "Seek counseling to treat your anxiety."

misbehave, she would punish us with silence. The bigger the infraction, the more she would ignore us. I made a promise that I would never treat people the way my mother treated us. To me, silence was cruel. Hit me, take away my privileges, but please don't ignore me!

I Teach What I Need to Learn Most

When my now grown daughter was 12 years old she misbehaved slightly, in a way that any healthy child might do. She truly was an admirable child, mind you. Even today, if there ever is a casting call in life for a "good person," she should be moved to the front of the line. So, this wonderful little girl had done something wrong. What did her loving father do about this? My reaction was inappropriate and immature—which is the point of the story.

Guess how I handled it? I shut down. If she spoke to me, I gave her short, curt responses. Otherwise, I remained very silent. Sound familiar? My wife, who may have been the first to notice the shift in my mood, asked, "Are you okay? Is something wrong?" I mumbled just enough words to cover my tracks.

The significant thing is, I was completely blind to my own behavior. I did not realize why or how I was acting. It was my daughter, who I inadvertently had been punishing for "hurting my feelings," who had the emotional honesty and courage to push past my initial denial. It took three attempts by her to get through to me with the question, "Are you upset with me?" It was the pain in her voice and tears in her eyes on the third try that woke me up to my passive-aggressive behavior. Anger was a "second emotion" for me in this instance. I felt angry, but below the anger I actually felt hurt.

The "child" in me came out. Unfortunately, and to my amazement, a reaction that I swore I would never perpetrate on anyone also came out: silence.

I never meant to hurt my daughter (See also Intention vs. Impact in Chapter 9.) I also did not intend for myself to suffer. Still, I chose to suffer. Why? I had adopted a bad theory, one that my mother demonstrated to me as a child, that this reaction of silence is what a good parent does when his/her feelings are hurt!

If you check off the items on the "To Suffer" side of Figure 8 on the next page, you will see that I hit the mother-load of unacceptable behavior, no pun intended. I was repeating the worst of the past. My silence was an ineffective ego-defense that I learned in my childhood, and a behavior I had sworn to never repeat.

One item in Figure 8 may need a bit of explaining: "Make the Irrational Rational," means that I made excuses and rationalized my behavior. "I know it doesn't make any sense and I realize that this is wrong, but I'm the father, which means that I deserve respect." In short, I attempted to justify my immature, inappropriate behavior.

If I wanted to handle the conflict without repeating the self-defeating drama from my early years, I would have instead realized, "I'm the adult, which means that I have to meet a higher standard. Children make mistakes and I need to "care-front"[9], not confront, the behavior with an appropriate response and not punish the person."

Choices We Make

To Suffer	To Live Authentically
Repeat negative, self-defeating attitudes and behaviors	Experience the pain required to change
Be defensive . . . make excuses	Live by lessons learned
Be what others want me to be (at the expense of my Self)	Live as I really am and who I "choose to be"
Make the irrational rational	Be compassionate
Hide in my comfort zone	Be grateful and live mindfully
Make excuses instead of changing my attitudes, habits and behaviors	Live, work and play BIG. Today is not a dress rehearsal. Celebrate life NOW . . .

Figure 8.

"Wounded Child"

What I did not fully realize at the time was that I had to go back in my lifeline to find the roots of my responses. I did not see it then, but in hindsight I realize that my wife was dangling the concept of a behavioral "MAP" in front of me. She asked, "What were you thinking? That's not like you." That is to say, "Why would you *choose* to shut your daughter out? What's the Motive?"

The "wounded child" in me came out when I became silent, as my mother had before me in similar situations. I went from victim to perpetrator. I've since found my brain (which at the time seemed to have fallen out) and have done a great deal of work to live more authentically. My journey into my self

---

9   To "care-front" someone means that I express a level of healthy anger/concern without forgetting the "main thing", which means that I do not damage the person's ego or in anyway undermine the relationship we share.

began with a great deal of pain. I realized that I had to let go of the past and re-examine old theories that protected me as a child in crisis, but were not serving me as an adult. I had to let go of the past in order to move on in my life.

I am a kind and compassionate person. I refused to go backward in my behavior by modeling old, self-defeating habits to punish people that I love and respect with my silence when they do something that upsets me. Today, I remain mindful of "keeping the main thing the main thing" (See Chapter 3.) And finally, I live and play **big**.

By big, I do not mean expensive. I mean passionately, with gusto, as if this moment is a miracle waiting to be celebrated.

Moving Away from Being the Victim

I'm fairly certain that you noticed that I did not tell you what occurred that allowed me to justify such a dark reaction to my daughter during the event I described. It's not because I do not want to share that with you, but because I don't remember! I can tell you that at the time, my daughter's behavior toward me *felt* like a big deal, like a knife in my heart. Remember, I was not thinking, which gave me the *excuse* to make the irrational rational. I was building a case to prove my core belief at the time, "Life is not fair. I am a victim."

In the past, I had spent a great deal of time in my life in the victim role. What is even worse, I expected people around me to read my mind. I'd imagine that some golden day they would wake up, shout, "Eureka!" and change their behavior. It was Dr. Mary Goldenson who gave me a wake up call. "Joe, no one is coming to rescue you," she said. "If they were, they'd have shown up by now. You can continue to suffer. Or, you can live the way you choose to live. You're reconstructing your past in the present. That doesn't make sense. Unless you choose to suffer."

This made perfect sense and had "opportunity" written all over it. Connecting the dots in my life was a commitment to live more authentically.

Connecting the Dots in My Life

Let's once again consider What … So What … Now What.

What: When I was four years old, my father was killed in an automobile accident. My mother took his death very hard, as she should, knowing how much she loved him and relied on him. Mom took ill and seemed to disappear. My brothers, one older and one younger than myself, and I were separated. I'm not sure how long we lived apart. I never asked and no one ever spoke about my father or the events that followed the accident. Silence was a family tradition.

So What: I learned to fend for myself. I falsely believed that I should not ask for what I desired. As crazy as it may sound (I made the irrational rational), I believed that asking for something that I desired was begging, and I was determined to prove that I was not a beggar.

Now What: Mom eventually found the strength to collect the three of us. We moved to Albany, New York and lived over my grandmother's grocery store. My dear mother worked her way up to a responsible position in the state tax division. She was a feminist long before women were burning their bras and demanding equal rights. She worked like a dog for my brothers and me, and never complained. Her way of showing love was to work hard and bring home the groceries; no whining, just get it done. Her job and the demands that came with raising three sons seemed to take her away all the time. It was as if she disappeared again.

My way of coping was to become independent and avoid being vulnerable. Unfortunately, I developed a number of life theories that protected my inner child at the time, but ultimately set me up for self-defeating behaviors later in life. I tended to show up in the role of the helper. That became my "Now What."

Changing the "Now What"

Years later, however, I wrote a personal manifesto as a declaration and personal commitment to change my behavior. Laurie Gerber and Juliana Gambrell, two incredible women who led a life-coaching series I attended, helped guide me through important blind spots.

Below is "My Manifesto." It may be a bit confusing. Don't get lost looking for the full content of the events following my dad's accident. "Listen" instead for the impact it had on me and how my self-defeating theories that resulted were shaping my behavior. I wrote this manifesto as part of a new life MAP, one that could help me avoid social-emotional dead ends and direct me through new life opportunities. I was tired of the circular route I was taking, repeating the pain of the past.

MY MANIFESTO

"You Gotta Love Him"

I have a clear life mission, one that has taken me on an incredible journey through Yesterday, Today and Tomorrow.

Yesterday was a very long and painful day for me. Scary events, one in particular, left me hoping that important people in my life would understand a clear and simple call for help: You gotta love this kid. After all, what's not to love about a beautiful four-year old child who is in big trouble?

Suffering came easy to me. I had a lot of practice. I can do suffering; it's living more authentically that I found tricky. Let's start from the beginning. You gotta empathize and let down your guard when you understand the circumstances that this kid had to face; I won't take advantage of it ... yet!

Life had safety and order and lots of country sunshine until that hot August night. One careless move by my father sent us into a tailspin, literally and figuratively. The crash wrecked the car and a whole lot of lives ... mine in particular. I learned a lot of things that night. For example, I didn't realize that people had funerals in their own homes. Who ever thought of that had to be weird. Dad's cold body was lying in a casket in full view of my bedroom. Aunt Sis told me he was sleeping, but I think I knew she was lying. Hey, I'm a kid, not a dumb kid. I kept playing a game with myself: Try not to look at Dad lying there so still. I dare you. No, I double dare.

I lost. I kept trying to see if he'd move. I also guess that I was hoping Aunt Sis was telling the truth. Adults don't do that a lot. They believe that a lie will protect kids. But a lie is a lie.

Oh, Mom disappeared that night too. I think she got sick, but I have no idea if she was in a hospital or hiding in the closet. I would have hidden there too, but it was too crowded. My truth began to take shape in a number of solid theories.

First, if I love you, you'll leave. Second, it does no good to wait. No one ever comes. And if they do, they come with food, lots of nice stuff, but they never talk about the things that matter. Like, where's Mom? And, is Dad really sleeping? If he is, when the hell is he going to wake up? I need him! Oh, that's the last time I remember thinking or saying those words, "I need."

Today is much better. I learned that there are payoffs if I do the care giving. After a long separation, I found my younger brother and took good care of him. I never did find my older brother. I think he's still buried deep in the closet. I learned to share everything except my vulnerability. My protective power-shield was best left up. I'd give you a skate key if you lost yours and a band-aid plus a hug if you fell.

I got so good at it that I eventually got more "keys". It felt good to nurture, protect and share my love with someone else. I've got a lot of love to give; but I don't need any for myself. I was working on sainthood and suffering quietly.

I sharpened my insight and life-theories and came at people with my version of care-frontation, part psychobabble from my psychology books, part gung-ho Marine Corps boot-camp credo: "When you're surrounded, **attack**."

Oh, did I mention, you **gotta** love this guy? You better, or he'll ask and challenge, or stare you down until you do. He is not afraid to share his thoughts and feelings. His world works in clear blacks and whites. Things make sense to him. **Don't you agree?**

He's tough to read, however. On the one hand, he can be very vulnerable; he's not afraid to cry or to share his deepest joy and pain. Without intending to do harm, he can make many adults uncomfortable with his intensity

Dr. Joe Currier

and passion for defining right vs. wrong. And you're supposed to read his mind if you really love him. He might even commit you if you don't. He has the keys, and the judgments to go with them. The good doctor developed a powerful, empathetic voice. But there was always an inner child still waiting.

Don't tell my dear friend, Carolyn, that I told you, but over the years, I brought a few nasty friends to ride shotgun on my occasional emotional drive-bys when I went out to prove my theories around my feelings of being unloved (or maybe my fears of being unlovable): Cowardly Chicken, Righteous Judge, and "Gunny", a Passionate Top Sergeant, who I always kept in the backseat (his presence could screw up the saint image and take away from my core message!):

You gotta love him! Sit up and listen. You **Gotta** Love Him. My care-frontation methodology occasionally omitted the care part of the message. I was really on a passionate mission. Truth … **My** Truth.

On one of my more memorable coaching visits into my SELF, I found another key: "I teach what I need to learn most." I had heard it before. It had been in the wind, but I was listening with my head. This time I felt it in my heart. I'm not sure if it was Carolyn whispering in my ear, or maybe my father came to me in a dream and told me that it was time to go on with my life. In any event, I heard it this time.

A new **self** showed up … a spirit-child who is on a mission and who is looking for volunteers. I am recruiting a legion of Guardian Angels, powerful individuals who love with grace and wisdom. My life's mission is: Leave No Child Behind—help heal the heart of the inner child.

But before I continue my journey, I think I'll sit back and listen for a while. First, listen to myself and the many voices from my past—some good and well intentioned, some just doing the very best they can. I also plan to listen deeply to my dear friend and life-traveler, Carolyn, who has shown up consistently not only to love me unconditionally, but also to teach me a critical life lesson, To live authentically and not hide my vulnerability just to prove a sad historical fact that "Bad things happen to good people."

It's no longer about being a victim to those events. It's about living and loving "big" because of them.

And to you, whoever's out there. I'm ready.

Oh, I have a new mantra, and it's the truth ... you'll see:

I gotta love you. I don't have a choice. It's who I am.

As I asked above, did you "listen" for the impact my dad's death had on me and how my self-defeating theories that resulted were shaping my behavior? I offer this personal example of "MAP"-ing my life, as others may MAP theirs. Bear with me as I explain in future pages.

CHAPTER 9

Here Comes the Judge

*"Every child is trying to live up
to his Father's expectations
or making up for his mistakes."*

—Barack Obama
44th President of the United States

Number One Salesman, But Not a Team Leader

Let me introduce you to Eli (not his real name, see Foreword), a 27-year-old senior salesman who was passed over for a promotion to a director-level managerial position. Members of the selection committee told Eli that he is very well admired as a producer, but that he is not valued as a partner or as a team leader.

Peers reported that they felt as if Eli thinks he is better than they are, and that he isolates himself. Behind his back, team members often mocked, "Here comes the judge," referring to Eli's sarcasm and dismissive facial set when peers made mistakes. Despite Eli's being the number one producer in this *Fortune 500* company, his immediate supervisor advised him that he would not be promoted until he changed his attitude and gained the support of his peers or those who reported to him (direct reports).

Eli was referred to me by the chairwoman of his company with a request "to help this young man explore what it means to lead". Eli was angry that he was not promoted and was convinced that his peers were simply jealous and vindictive. He also initially showed no interest in my executive coaching process nor any insight into the "at risk" effects of his life history before we began to "MAP" his behavior.

Intention vs. Impact

Very early in our coaching relationship I sensed that Eli was in denial regarding the feedback he received. He told me that he was only doing what he had been taught by his dad, which was to work hard, keep your head down, and mind your business. Eli said his father told him, "If you do that, people will notice, and promotions will follow." Eli also had been taught that being promoted to a leadership position came when you proved yourself to be the best. "And I am the best," he said. "No brag, just fact."

I took this opportunity to jump in with my opinion. "The numbers prove it: you are the best salesperson in the company," I said. "My question is, Are you the best partner in the organization?"

At Risk Achiever	POWER Performer
Good to excellent at one's job, BUT does not reflect core cultural values.	Meets or exceeds performance goals AND reflects core cultural values.
Misaligned Underachiever	Loyal Underachiever
Poor performance AND does not reflect core cultural values.	Fails to meet performance goals, but does reflect core cultural values.

Culture Fit: Do you live the values?
FIGURE 9: Performance - Culture Model

I showed Eli Figure 9 and asked him where he thought he belonged in the Performance-Culture Model. He seemed genuinely intrigued by the question.

Without much hesitation, Eli identified himself as an "At-Risk Achiever." He produced significant revenue for the organization, but little else. He admitted that he did not put the same effort into leading and promoting cultural norms as he did selling. He was certainly not a "POWER" player (See Chapter 4: Passion-Ownership-Wellness-Excellence-Relationships) because he lacked a sense of ownership and did very little to build meaningful relationships with peers and direct reports.

Eli had a very narrowly focused explanation for his leadership omissions. "I'm a worker bee, not a leader!," he explained. "That's John Doe's job; he's the Regional Manager. I'm trying to earn the promotion, but have not been given the title yet." I was quick to suggest that "leading" is not about having a title. I told him that leadership is the opportunity of everyone in an organization who can add value in the moment. And ownership does not come with a stock certificate; it comes with a spirit of concern and responsibility. It's every team member's obligation to reflect the core cultural values, which in Eli's company were very clearly stated as, Unite and conquer the competition.

Eli repeatedly missed the opportunity to lead, which is the reason his senior associates hesitated to promote him. His boss even cautioned him. "The people who would have to follow you if you were promoted to a leadership position say that you are mean-spirited and self-centered," he told Eli "They don't think you care about them or the company."

Caring vs. Showing You Care

Eli was very difficult to read. For example, I was not sure what he was thinking or feeling when I told him about the advice that my dear friend Dr. Leslie

Frankfurt once told me, a strategy that I believe every passionate, upwardly mobile executive might well heed:

> **"People don't care how much you know**
> **until they know how much you care!"**

Eli was quick to retort, "I care a lot. That's why I work so hard. And I'm not mean. I don't have a mean bone in my body!"

I believed him. "I apologize," I said. "I don't want to hurt your feelings. I believe that you're a good person with good intentions. Good intentions may get you into heaven, but they will not get you into a leadership position, however. Leaders must understand and manage the impact they create. People have been trying to tell you that they will not follow you just because of your expertise."

Up to this point, our executive coaching relationship seemed more like a visit to a dentist than a collaboration. I felt that I had to pull any thoughts and feelings from him as if I were extracting a tooth. This conversation was the first time that I felt that we were truly engaged in a meaningful dialogue.

CONNECT THE DOTS...

Eli, a 27-year old top salesperson, is unclear as to why he was passed over for a promotion. According to him, his sales numbers should have been his ticket to the promotion. I suggested that he might be caught in a vicious cycle, probably as a result of life marker events.

Connect the Dots: Eli's MAP

Eli reported that his life history was "fairly ordinary". He did not feel that there were any noteworthy events in his younger years that would account for his business mishaps. His story suggested differently.

What?

When Eli was eleven years old, his father, a construction laborer who made his living scaling scaffolds and steel beams, slipped on a patch of ice, fell twenty feet, and broke his leg and collarbone.

So What?

Although he never shared it at the time, years later, his dad confessed a sense of shame and recalled feeling weak and a burden to his family. "Real men are providers, not bed-ridden invalids," his father said. His father's entire identity was wrapped up in being the breadwinner. Eli's dad never showed his emotions, a habit that he had learned from his father before him. Eli reported that his dad was especially quiet during his rehabilitation. "I remember being afraid to go near him," Eli recalled. "He just stared out the window."

At one point, Eli and his sisters believed that their father was terminally ill because everyone whispered about his medical condition. They did not know that people were more worried that he would drink himself to death since he was depressed over the fact that he could not provide for his family.

Lessons Learned

In his early years, the damaging lessons that Eli learned, which became his underlying beliefs, included:

- ✓ **Never** show your emotions.

- ✓ Vulnerability is a sign of weakness.

- ✓ 'Good' parents are 'strong' people who suck it up.

- ✓ Hard work is how a spouse and parent show love.

Now What?

Eli repeated a silent pledge his dad had made: "When I get back on my feet, I'll work harder and never complain."

Play it again, Sam … FAMILY LINEAGE

Children operate in the "shadow" of their early marker events, as well as those of their parents. Children initially define their world through the eyes of elders, people they literally look UP to. There is also DNA, which tends to retain certain trait patterns.

What?

When his dad lost his job when Eli was eleven years old, the family had to go on welfare. The food stamps Eli had to use at lunchtime at school were a bright red color, symbolically shouting to the kids in line, "Here's a beggar; give him a handout. Poor boy!" it seemed to Eli.

So What?

Eli was embarrassed and felt ashamed. Kids taunted him in the cafeteria. He also felt that everyone stared at him in the supermarket when his mom handed the clerk food stamps. He never told his parents about his discomfort or conflict. He emulated them, acting strong, and just "sucked it up."

More Lessons Learned?

- ✓ "Vulnerability is a sign of weakness, a luxury I can't afford!"

- ✓ Wealth means you are 'somebody.'

- ✓ Work hard. If that doesn't work, Work Harder. If that doesn't work, **Work Even Harder!!**

- ✓ Monetary success is the "main thing"-- $$$$$$$$$$$$$$

- ✓ Remain vigilant. You never know when tragedy will strike or the bottom will fall out. There is never enough money!

Now What?

Eli had made a private promise to himself: "No one will ever laugh at me again. I will be successful (success meant wealthy)."

The truth is, once Eli's father recovered from his scaffolding accident, he actually did not hammer him with doom-and-gloom messages filled with threats like, "Work hard or else!" In fact, Eli did not recall his dad telling him much of anything. "My dad was a very quiet man," Eli recounted. "He worked all the time. Even when he got home, he kept himself busy. He seemed driven, as if he'd die if he slowed down and enjoyed life." It was the painful look in his dad's eyes that caused Eli to model his behavior, work, Work, **WORK**.

If we "MAP" Eli's behavior, what Motivates him? Is he simply a rising star with a strong work ethic, someone who strives for self-expression and hopes to earn a spot on a power performance team? That would suggest that he is motivated by Social (Level III), Psychological (Level IV) and, at times, even Self-Actualization (Level V) needs on the Hierarchy of Human Needs (See Chapter 6).

It would be reasonable to believe that Eli was simply a dedicated worker, and devoted father and spouse to his family. It would be reasonable, yet incorrect!

Rather, Eli was driven by Level I and II needs, the need for security and the need for recognition. He lived in fear that economic calamity, followed by mocking stares and snide whispers, lurked in the imaginary minefield of business and life. Monetary success created an illusion of safety and self-worth. He lived in the emotional shadows of his early shame and social embarrassment. Eli recalled his pain and humiliation when peers called him and his family "trailer-park trash."

CONSIDER THIS

There is a difference between
BEING successful and FEELING successful

How Eli Saw Himself

After a brief thoughtful deliberation, Eli agreed with my suggestion that the problem was **not** so much the painful reminders of being labeled. The real problem was that he **believed** the labels!!

Business success did not diminish Eli's shame or help him avoid unhealthy competition. Eli was on a misguided mission to prove his self-worth. Despite his desire to lead, he could not get past himself long enough to lead others.

How Others Saw Eli

Eli's co-workers described him as an unforgiving perfectionist. They admired his work ethic, but were afraid that they could not keep up with him. People also resented his snide comments and harsh criticisms when they did not live up to **his** standards. People who liked Eli feared that they would eventually let him down, thus avoided partnering with him. His wife sometimes wished she worked for him, at least to get his attention. She often complained, "If I worked for you, you'd treat me better and I'd see you more."

Eli, meanwhile, was like a coal miner —with tunnel vision! —who was so busy working in the dark that he did not realize that the canary was dead and that he is in an "at risk" situation both at home and at work. It was as if he sucked the oxygen out of relationships with his constant drive for perfection and self-focus. You might say his slogan could be, "Good enough is never good enough!"

How's It Working For You?

Eli literally cried, maybe for the first time in his life, when I asked him the question, "So, how's it working for you?"

I was quick to let him know that I was extremely impressed with the vulnerability he showed when he finally shared his sadness and pain. On a more task-related note, I told him that I believed that he was operating with a few outdated, self-defeating theories that he might want to rethink if he was to become the husband, father, son, and leader that he hoped to be.

Say no more ... Eli began to put his passion to work for him, his family, and his team! Eli had not only achieved the next step along the career path, soon after, he was nominated by his peers and promoted as a Regional Vice President.

When he completed the coaching process, Eli remarked, "I'd give a million dollars if my dad could have had someone like my corporate partners who cared enough to invest in **his** life. My dad is still climbing scaffolds and lives with a fear that he won't be able to provide for my mom and younger sister. He laughs when I tell him what we talk about. I told him recently, 'You can laugh, but you can't hide. I'm coming after you!'"

Eli's departing words to me were, "Oh, you should have seen my dear father suck back his tears when I told him that I love and admire him." Eli has still never heard his father say those three magical words in return, but he's still hopeful.

Until he does hear them, I encouraged him to keep reaching out and speaking his truth ... from his head and his heart!

The Power of "R" (Relationships) ... From the dinner table to the boardroom to the athletic arena

While I was congratulating Jim Fassel for his United Football League (UFL) championship victory as Head Coach of the *Las Vegas Locomotives*, he reminded me of the quote that I had shared while he was facing adversity as the Offensive Coordinator of the Baltimore Ravens, a time when some players believed that Jim only cared about their performance on the field:

> *"People don't care how much you **KNOW**
> until they know how much you **CARE**."*

The coach went on to say, "*I opened and closed the season with this message. It's my job as a team leader to let players and staff know that our partnership goes beyond the gridiron statistics and the number of wins versus losses. I'm responsible for their well-being, celebrate their best efforts and offer them support, guidance, and a loving kick-in-the-ass when they're not fully focused.*"

Coach Fassel stands head-to-head with other *power leaders* who go beyond the mere drive to win ... he gives a damn about the individuals who struggle to complete the mission.

CHAPTER 10

DUM, Not Dumb!

Question:

**Why do people like Eli
repeat behaviors that
do not pay off?**

**They are DUM, but not dumb!
!**

That's "DUM"!

If you wonder why people repeat self-defeating behavior, it's not because they're dumb (ignorant), but because they are "DUM": I Don't Understand the Meaning.

Variations of acting DUM[10] include things like:

"Sorry ... That is not what I meant to say/do."

"Wow ... That was not my intention."

"Oops ... That came out wrong. Let me try again."

Acting DUM is not a sign of personal ignorance, but it can be perceived poorly by others.

Remember, perception may not be accurate, but it is what causes people to form judgments and react as they do.

When individuals act DUM, they are at risk for toxic reactions. Remember Eli from the previous chapter? In Eli's case, he was flying blind. By not "connecting the dots" in his life, he did not understand what truly motivates him, nor the impact of his behavior on other people, including his family.

Eli's intentions were good—he wanted to be a proper provider (like his father) and keep himself and his family safe and comfortable. He misinterpreted the looks on the faces of peer-partners and blocked out the feedback of his superiors when they told him that he's pushing people too hard. His mantra, "I never ask them to do anything that I would not do myself," was a form of denial to excuse the trail of bodies he left behind in his competitive wake.

Old Habits Die Hard

"I can't help how I think," Eli reasoned. "It was good enough for Dad, so it's good enough for me. It's not my nature to confront people. Real men don't cry. I've never been able to speak in front of large groups. It's always been this way ..."

These may seem like good excuses, but they are excuses all the same. Old practices—attitudes, habits and behaviors—are difficult to break. The questions are: Are they based on ineffective theories that no longer serve you? Are they based on beliefs that lock you into self-limiting behaviors?

---

10   For more information, see Glossary of Terms and Text References at back.

It was difficult and sometimes confusing for Eli to "connect the dots" in his life and accept the fact that he was living and working in a fear-driven "survival" mode, rather than a more healthy competitive "prosper" mode. Embedded in his childhood's nightmarish memories was the worry that he could end up like his dad—poor, out of control, the butt of people's pitying jokes, and "trailer park trash" stares.

"Necessary" Lies?

Men and women like Eli may continue to be victimized by their self-defeating thoughts and behaviors until they connect the dots and build bridges from traumatic marker events to more constructive alternatives. Otherwise, they will continue to internalize "necessary lies" to justify their controlling attitudes and behaviors that weaken partnership bonds at work and at home.

Necessary lies are excuses offered to justify negative behavior. One example is when Eli rationalizes his rigid, controlling, critical actions as an expression of his work ethic. Another example is when a high-potential executive attempted to justify her life-long insecurity with a promise to slow down and chill out as soon as she is promoted and more financially solvent. The truth is she will never feel more relaxed. She'll find something else to worry about. Eli and she told what they believe are necessary lies, not even realizing they are lying to themselves in fact.

Nature or Nurture?

In his book, "The Biology of Belief," Dr. Bruce Lipton raises the bar regarding what behaviors we can and cannot change. He is one of the many scientific scholars engaged in cell-biology research whose data show that humans do have the ability to change, and even reverse, some of their genetic blueprints.

According to Dr. Lipton, life is *not* determined by genes. In fact, his research has led to the conclusion that genes are simply biological blueprints. The encouraging news is that the research by Lipton and others suggest that our personal belief systems, including our perceptions, have the capacity to trump our genetic inheritance and our cellular DNA. When we change the way we think, and learn new ways to "size up" situations, we can actually alter our reactive habits and DNA.

Psychologist and best-selling author Dr. Wayne Dyer highlights the "Placebo Effect" as further evidence that our beliefs can and do control our biology. Documented studies showed that sugar pills given to a control group believing that they were being given a remedy for, say, arthritis, turn out to be as effective as the drug being administered for the treatment of that ailment. This placebo effect occurs due to a belief in the effectiveness of the pill.

Author James Allen offers a narrative point of view: "We do not attract that which we want, but that which we are."

Dr. Dyer's personal philosophy is: "Who I am is first and foremost determined by what I believe—and that leads me to consciously focus on the fact that limitations or traits inherited from my ancestors are absolutely not the final word."

The Meme Virus (Meme rhymes with Team)

Another way we often use "necessary lies" to justify our self-defeating behavior comes from Dr. Dyer's "Excuses Begone" work. "In addition to our genetic makeup," Dr. Dyer recounts, "the other big excuse that most of us use to justify unhappiness, poor health, and a lack of success is the family and cultural conditioning we've been programmed with." Dr. Dyer notes the impact in our lives of "memes," a term coined by Dr. Richard Dawkins in his book, "The Selfish Gene."

Memes or memetics come from the word mimic, which means to observe and copy behavior. Just like a gene is the basic unit of genetics, the basic unit of memetics is a meme. However, unlike an atom, a meme has no physical properties. Memes are embedded in our recurring thoughts, not in our DNA.

Dr. Richard Brodie in his work, "Virus of the Mind," says that a meme is an attitude, thought or belief in the mind that can spread to and from other people's minds. The research shows that by the age of six or seven, all of us have been programmed with a massive inventory of memes that act like a virus. Attitudes, thoughts and behaviors are repeated and passed on to others, like a virus spreads from person to person in the cold and flu season.

Once a meme is in our mind, it can and will both consciously and subliminally influence our behavior. This is one way that human beings acquire a huge cache of excuses and alibis that keep us in our behavioral rut. Dr. Brodie emphasizes the viral nature of historic memories and describes what happens in the mind through mimicking, modeling and imitating. He notes that the nature of a virus is to reproduce itself ... to make copies of itself as often as possible and to penetrate all available openings, thus spreading itself to as many hosts as possible.

Special memories die hard because they become who we think we are. Core beliefs (such as "I'm a pessimist; I've always looked at life through a half-empty perspective") die hard because they are memetically fixed in our minds to the point that they form a part of our identity. These beliefs gradually spread throughout our social milieu and form filters of how people perceive us.

When it comes to changing my behavior, and, if I am to mimic Maslow's self-actualizing legacy of "I must be all that I can be," I cannot afford to hide in these and other powerful excuses. They're still excuses, i.e., **choices** that I make in the moment.

Dr. James Allen challenges us to change our life's direction:

"By changing my beliefs, I change who I am."

Here's a suggestion:

Love your parents and the many people who taught you their version of "What is." *But,* please don't stay trapped in DUM behavior ... **You are better than that!**

"If you correct your mind,
the rest of your life will fall into place."

—Lao-Tzu

CHAPTER 11

Your Childhood Is Over . . . But It May Not Be Complete

When Hard Work is Not Working

Let me introduce Peter (not his real name, see Foreword), a Million Dollar Roundtable sales association winner for the past ten years. His career journey is a variation of the message Eli received—hard work pays off. As we attempted to MAP Peter's life-journey, he became surprised by some of the hidden agendas in his back-story. His professional colleagues also were shocked when they finally came to know what drove this incredible man.

An upwardly mobile middle manager, Peter is what I refer to as an "At-Risk Achiever" (see Chapter 9). He has very strong business skills, meets and exceeds performance expectations, but does not reflect the core cultural values of his organization.

Abusive Management Style?

Peter was known as "the Corporate Terminator," a tough, no-nonsense manager who did not tolerate people who complained or made excuses. He never asked anyone to do anything that he would not do himself. Peter insisted, "People who do not succeed are lazy or uncommitted." His formula for success was simple: "Work hard. If that does not achieve your goal, work harder. If that does not achieve your goal, work even harder!"

For years, managers have tolerated his abusive behavior because they knew that he was a good man who never intended to belittle people. Managers repeatedly turned a blind eye to those direct reports and peer-partners who refused to work with Peter. They would rationalize the complaints by saying, "You know Peter! He's such a passionate guy. We just have to find people who fit his style."

Peter had no tolerance for anyone who *he believed* was not passionate. He was proud to say, "I drive people out of the company if they do not show me what I need to see." Co-workers often asked each other, "What's with Peter? What drives his behavior?" The answer usually harkened back to his days as a winning hockey player— "He plays hard and likes to win. Anything short of best effort kills him."

What people did not know is that Peter operated in the shadow of his early academic experiences. The truth is that Peter has a severe learning disability. He is dyslexic. Peter hid the fact that he cannot read well, and lived in constant terror that people would discover his disability, and then consider him to be dumb. No matter how much money he made and how many accolades he received as the result of the sales numbers he posted, Peter struggled with impostor fears (or the imposter syndrome). He worried that if people knew the truth about his disability they would expose his limitations.

As I listened respectfully to Peter's story, I told him, "I do not believe that your major problem is related to the idea that people might think you are dumb if they knew that you could not read well. I think the real issue is that *you* believe you are dumb! I worry that you are ashamed and disappointed with yourself. I also believe that you think you've let your family down." He did not respond to my statement. Instead, he focused on the feelings he had toward his father, a man that he looked up to and from whom he struggled to earn respect. "I always let my father down," Peter confided. "I was the bad penny of the family, a loser."

"Wow," I countered. "What did you say when your father called you a loser and when you let him down?"

"He never actually called me a loser," Peter responded. "I felt like a loser! My parents always said, 'Do your best. Give it everything you got. Then, whether you win or lose, shake it off and move on.'" Then he added, "But they *had* to say that."

"Peter, if I heard you correctly, you've been making up nasty stories about yourself in your mind," I told him. "It's your shame, not your father's disappointment that's driving you so hard."

Peter, however, was not about to let himself off so easily! Instead, he insisted, "My dad *must* be embarrassed by me! I have a brother who's a successful attorney, and a sister who is raising a wonderful family *and* is a professor at Columbia University. My dad also stands out in our community. I'm the village idiot. I can't even read."

"I'm not interested in a sibling 'academic performance-beauty-contest,' and I am not here to judge you," I told him. It's your shame that worries me. I think you're on a mission to *prove* that you're a loser. Your corporate kamikaze behavior is what I'm trying to understand. You use competitive opportunities like weapons to beat down the competition."

Connect the Dots

Peter, a 41 year-old sales rep, has a reputation for burning people out, for being a corporate bully. Yet, he is trying to earn a spot on the management team, which has been a major struggle for him. Let's MAP his behavior:

Motivation	And	Perception
Peter is struggling with deep self-esteem issues and is trying to earn the respect of people he hopes to affiliate with. He describes himself as a Corporate Athlete competing to win. I propose that he is a competitive bully struggling to prove that he is not a loser! Negative Level III (social) and IV (psychological) needs.	**WHAT** Significant Life Events * **SO WHAT** Lessons Learned * **NOW WHAT** How I show up in the current event	Peter is certain that he is an embarrassment to his family. He believes that people would judge him and laugh at him if they knew his secret. He beats them to the punch by outworking them, thereby seemingly justifying his "in your face" behavior.

*See Chapter 6, **Maslow's Hierarchy of Human Needs**

Proving Himself Proved Ineffective

Peter's career-journey to the top of his organization was hijacked by his need to prove his self-worth. He is an "At-Risk Achiever," who consistently creates profitability, but at a negative cost to both institutional culture and partnerships. He does not teach, coach or mentor. Instead, he judges people. When they made <u>DUM</u> mistakes or lacked confidence in the face of conflict, Peter looked at them with the same look he saw (or imagined) when he stood in front of the class and could not read. He's quick to label people as lazy and unmotivated. Work associates have been trying to tell him that he is a "performance bully" who shames people by not only outworking them, but also by shooting them a sarcastic "in your face" smirk when he wins.

It's interesting how Peter often distorted the facts when it came to his historic record. He minimized his athletic and business performance, acting as if just anyone could excel as a Division I hockey competitor. What also stood out to me about him was that Peter's unique power was tucked away in the very shadow that he tried to hide behind. There are many high achievers who— with the right education, experience, executive coaching and dedication— have made it to the Million Dollar Roundtable, but how many have done so despite having the burden of a significant learning disability? I would venture to say not many. That is unusual!

A Similar Story

I told Peter that he reminded me of another man I know, a man whom I deeply admire, a man who was not learning disabled, but was socially handicapped. I use the word "handicapped" not in a dark, sinister, crippling manner, but to denote that he was burdened with impostor fears as a result of the "sins of the father" and a rigid British class system.

This exceptional man's race up the career ladder was weighted down in a manner similar to a racehorse to which handicappers assign additional weight prior to a steeplechase. The man I am referring to is Simon Robinson, President of Major, Lindsey and Africa, the premier legal staffing organization. MLA is noted for its Ivy League pedigree. Degrees hang on its corporate walls from Harvard, Princeton, Stanford and nearly every other prestigious institution. I will leave Mr. Robinson to tell his own story, but unlike so many others in the firm he ran, he got his education in the school of hard knocks.

When Mr. Robinson called me, it was with a request to write him a recommendation for an MBA program that he was preparing to enroll in at the beginning of the upcoming academic year. It made perfect sense to solidify his executive credentials. He did **not** say it, but I imagined that some of his business colleagues might have been wondering how a man such as Mr. Robinson could lead such a prestigious organization without the traditional academic background.

Here's my take on the situation: Many people have a chance to be named president of a distinguished, academically-based organization when they come armed with an MBA degree, but *just imagine* someone who had to climb the ivy covered walls of industry with a high school education and a story to tell! I do not know about you … but that's a man I want to meet and follow!

I trusted that Peter would not misinterpret my message. This is not about whether Mr. Robinson chose to pursue a formal academic degree to back up his already proven business prowess. It was about Mr. Robinson's having the "smarts" in the form of innate intelligence, character, and the ability to prosper in the face of conflict. And beyond these POWER characteristics as a leader, Mr. Robinson keeps his executive eye on the "main thing." (See Chapter 4 — Passion-Ownership-Wellness-Excellence-Relationships.)

Mr. Robinson once told me that his primary leadership objective is to give people at work a better experience. "I need to treat people well and teach them to treat other people well," he told me. He creates a partnership-chain, of "Tag, you're it".

A Similar Challenge

Having realized that Peter was just as unusual as Mr. Robinson, I told him, "Peter, you are special. To achieve what you have achieved under such extraordinary circumstances will get people to sit up and listen if you'd stop barking at them and stop hiding your true self. I imagine that your dad loves all three of his children, including you. But, if you ask me, I believe that he must have a special respect and appreciation for your achievements. I think it's time to stop kicking yourself in the ass and **lead** your team. That's your next challenge."

Completing Childhood

Many of us are in a similar boat as Peter. We carry unproductive baggage from our childhoods in the form of bad theories and self-defeating beliefs that slow us down and get us off course.

Remember the title of this chapter? Our Childhood Is Over, But It May Not Be Complete! For Peter, it is time to complete his childhood. How does he do this? One way is to reexamine the "So What" that arises from the dramatic marker events he experienced on his life journey. Peter might ask, **"So What, I have a learning disability!** So what does that mean? Does it mean that I'm dumb?" That's an emotional excuse to deflect the fact that Peter chose to hold on to and to carry the negative comments that kids hurled at him when, as a dyslexic, he could not distinguish between the letters "b" and "d."

Consider the facts from Peter's perspective: "I have trouble reading. My constructive opportunity is to explore, 'So What' can I do to absorb important information? Do I fall back on my strong auditory skills? Do I ask for untimed testing?"

There are a host of valuable "So What" questions that can solve a problem versus dragging his ego through the mud as he had been doing to himself.

I left Peter with a message from on high, or nearly on high, since I saw the message on a bumper sticker on the back of a taxi while crossing the street in downtown Milwaukee years ago. Hey, what more evidence do you need that this message is the real deal? It was on a taxi bumper in Milwaukee! Here goes:

**It's Never Too Late
To Have a Happy Childhood!**

CHAPTER 12
Sins of the Father

Do You Believe All This Stuff?

Jay (not his real name, see Foreword) is a man I first met while I was leading a team-building workshop. During a break in the session, Jay came up to me and asked, "Do you really believe all this stuff you talk about? Do you think you're always right?" Judging by his tone, of course, Jay probably meant to say, "all this bull----," so I tried to bring some levity to my response.

"Yes," I said, "except for the part about me always being right. My wife insists I was wrong in 1969, '71, and '99. I agree with '69 and '71, but still dispute 1999. Why do you ask?" Although I thought I was being hilarious, Jay did not smile. I was hoping that humor might reduce any tension, gambling that he would not see my response as sarcastic (Intent vs. Impact, you know! - See Chapter 9.).

"You keep insisting that people are feeling something as if there is an automatic emotions trip-switch," Jay said, adding that he did not agree, that he did not react that way. "I believe that I'm like Janet (a co-worker in the meeting who told the group that she is non-confrontational by nature). I just don't get upset."

"Are you telling me that you *never* get angry?" I asked him.

"That's right," he said. "I do not get angry. Anger *never* solves anything. I learned as a kid that it doesn't get you anywhere but in trouble."

Primary Emotions

Jay patiently waited while I drew two diagrams (see Figure 10). "The research is indisputable," I told him. ***All human beings*** are born with four primary emotions. I use the term 'primary,' because they are hard-wired into the brain. We smile when happy. We feel discomfort and, at times, even cry when we're sad and in pain. We prepare to withdraw to protect ourselves when we sense fear. And, we puff up, get loud and step forward, ready for action, when we're angry."

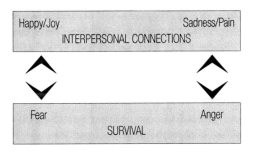

Figure 10: Primary Human Emotions

I paused to check Jay's response before continuing. He said nothing so I added, "The word 'we' is meant to include you too, Jay." He just grimaced as if he knew something that I did not know. And he did. In my opinion, Jay has memories of marker events that taught him to override some primary emotions.

As the diagram indicates, all human beings have four primary emotions. Primary emotions come with our birth certificates. Over time, perhaps with much scolding, shaming, and punishing from our parents, we can redirect these feelings, and can come to deny they exist and hide them under the carpet in our homes and offices. Still, they are there!

When I say that emotions can be redirected, I mean that they can be mislabeled and reinterpreted. Let's consider the emotion of anger. Anger is often redirected or reinterpreted as a 'second emotion'—a second emotion expressed when we don't or feel we can't express the first emotion. For example, I might feel hurt when a girlfriend breaks up with me, but hesitate to show that hurt, and my vulnerability. I might also be afraid that she would take advantage of the power I attribute to her if I showed my true emotions, so I might puff out my chest and attempt to achieve illusions of control and shreds of dignity by telling her, "Get lost! I don't care." My words and behavior portray anger, but the truth is the primary emotion I feel is sadness/pain.

At a very early age, most males are sent the message that "real men don't cry." They begin early to shake off fear and sadness. Take the example of a child afraid of an immunization injection, panic stricken at the thought of it, who begins to cry. A well-intentioned parent may try to toughen that child up and admonish, "Keep it up and I'll give you something to really cry about." Or, take the example of young athletes, when injured. They may need to comply with the macho warnings of their coaches reverberating throughout the locker room, "Don't be a baby; rub some dirt on it."

Emotions both unite and protect us. Two sets of emotions—Happiness/Joy and Sadness/Pain—unite us. They are meant to connect us to each other. We are social animals, plus there is strength in numbers. Two others are designed to protect us—Anger and Fear. These are key parts of the "fight-or-flight" survival mechanism.

Range of Emotions

There are hundreds of words to describe the range of these four primary emotions, but they all boil down to the same messages. There are performance and social pay-offs when we unite in a team, and survival benefits when we react against to dangers in the environment.[11]

- **Happiness/Joy** ranges from amused to ecstatic ... Life is working for me; I am content.

- **Sadness/Pain** may show up from uncomfortable to devastated ... I feel as if I'm losing something; life hurts.

- **Anger** may weigh in from annoyed to enraged ... Something is upsetting me; I better do something about it.

- **Fear** may sneak a peak from anxious to terrorized ... Something is overwhelming me; I'd better withdraw to a safer position.

Like it or not, emotions are natural human reactions that show up when specific situations grab our instinctive attention. What I do about the emotions, however, is under my control, including denying my feelings by sweeping them under a carpet. When I do not react to emotional conflicts, for example, by not confronting someone who has crossed the line in my eyes, it is *not* that I am incapable of getting angry. Instead, it may be that I do not want to *feel* the discomfort of reacting strongly or do not wish to *face* the consequences if I react.

Back to Jay & the Diagram

I could see that I was not dazzling Jay with my drawing or my point of view, so I asked him if we could take a walk down his memory lane and MAP his behavior. He thought it was a waste of time, but he agreed.

---

11   Credit is due here to my associate, Jim Mitchell, for this particular primary emotions model. Jim has a wonderful way of adding a unique interpretation to the research.

Dr. Joe Currier

I asked him to list three words that describe an important person in his life. Without a moment of hesitation, Jay replied, "My dad -- angry, abusive, controlling." I asked him to think of a marker event that might illustrate his dad's pattern of behavior. He shared a hotspot in his family history. "My dad is always in control. He dominates my Mother, which upsets me." And, according to Jay, his father would often fly off the handle at the slightest provocation.

"Point to which of these four emotions (Figure 10) you're referring to when you allowed your dad to upset you," I asked Jay. He just stared at the model and said nothing.

"Jay," I prodded him, "I'm suggesting that you were feeling one or more of these emotions when you recall a specific reaction by your dad. Please describe a specific event and tell me what you were feeling. If you don't know or cannot remember, just make it up like a movie director coaching an actor in a drama."

I sensed that Jay had stepped into a powerful memory. He looked like a deer paralyzed by the blinding lights of an oncoming tractor-trailer. Jay began to recall and recount a terrorizing situation he experienced at the age of eight years old. He woke from a sound sleep to the shouts of his parents. They were arguing downstairs. They did not know he was awake, but Jay quietly perched himself at the top of the stairs. He came in at the tail-end of the battle only to witness his father screaming an obscenity. His mother was crying, and pleaded with her husband, "Calm down. I'm sorry. I'm sorry."

In Jay's memory, his mom said nothing else. She just kept crying and pleading, and taking the blame.

Then Jay became panicky when recalling the next rapid-fire memory. His dad slammed his fist into the front door, shattering the glass panel, and stormed out. His mom ran on to the driveway and watched helplessly as he got into the car and drove away. Neither parent was aware that Jay witnessed their battle, or that he slinked away and slept at the foot of his older sister's bed, fearing that neither parent would be there when he woke up.

Jay eventually identified his emotion as fear. Still, he denied any anger at his father or the situation he faced as a child. I was not trying to justify, or in any way minimize the impact of his father's behavior when I asked him if there might not be some misinterpretation of what happened. He insisted that this was typical, however. He said his dad was bullying his mom and she was apologizing for something that she never should have apologized for. His mom was a victim; his dad was a bully.

I told Jay that I was trying to put myself in his place, and in my own mind began to see myself as if I was an eight-year-old child who accidentally parachuted into a powerful family psychodrama. I imagined that I would be very frightened in the moment, especially having been awakened from a deep sleep. I also believe that I would be upset and disappointed with my father for overreacting to whatever my mom may have done. I would *not* stop loving him; he's my father, but I'd feel *angry* and would wish that I felt safe enough to say to him, "Please stop what you're doing. You're scaring me and you're hurting Mom."

Jay stared at me as if I were speaking politically correct? How about speaking in tongues or a foreign language? When I pushed him to get in touch with the *possibility* that he may have felt angry, he said, "No. You're wrong," which he repeated insistently twice more. I was about to offer a further perspective when he raised his voice in an impassioned plea, "Leave me alone," he said. "What the hell is wrong with you? Are you telling me to punch my father??!!"

His response did not surprise me. I understood his confusion facing the paradox of "how I feel" versus "what I do" in experiencing such strong emotions.

"No, I don't want you to raise your hands to your father," I assured him. "Your feelings are different from your actions. You can *feel* angry and still choose not to hurt someone. Just because you walk away from a conflict by suppressing your anger, or sweep rage under the rug does not change or diminish the fact that you feel something. You were frightened, confused, *and angry*. That is what any normal eight-year-old child would feel."

Jay seemed to have enough. I could not read what he was thinking or feeling, but I did sense that it was time to stop for now. I asked him a final question: "What did your mom and dad say when you finally told them that you were carrying around this painful memory?"

I frequently ask the question, "What did he say when you told him that?" People are often unaware of the impact they are creating and remain in a blind window until someone cares enough to tell them how their actions are perceived, in this case, when a child tells a parent how a remembered incident affected them. Jay's response? "I never told them," he said finally, and walked away from me.

Misinterpreting Lessons Learned

Most of us have been involved in an ugly and regretted, over-reactive situation that would have scared the hell out of our children if they had been sitting at the top of the stairs witnessing it. If you were the child who did witness such a 'gory' battle-scene between people you love, it would be easy to misinterpret the "lessons learned" from it.

A few examples of misinterpretations would be:

- ✓ All fighting is bad.

- ✓ Fighting is a waste of time.

- ✓ Good people don't get angry.

- ✓ Couples in loving relationships never fight.

Connect the Dots

Jay is an upwardly mobile executive who describes himself as naturally quiet and non-confrontational. His lack of assertiveness could derail his career aspirations. He also reports that he would like to improve his relationship with his father, a man that he describes as a bully.

Jay operated under each of the above misinterpretations or false assumptions. He was attempting to avoid the perceived "sins of the father" by adopting a 180 degree-opposing style. Truth is, his lack of response to difficult situations was as ineffective as his dad's overreaction. His father's hostility was damaging to both family relationships and to Jay's self-esteem. Jay's silence was a passive response to a crisis, which actually cried out for support and resolution.

Jay's MAP

If we <u>MAP</u> Jay's behavior, we see that he seeks safety and comfort (Level II - Safety) and needs for affiliation (Level III - Social) in the face of confrontation (See Chapter 6, Maslow's Hierarchy of Human Needs.) It is important to his self-image (Level IV - Psychological) to **not** react like his father did during marital difficulties or other challenging situations.

Jay's reactions, or lack thereof, do nothing to manage tension or bring closure to painful events. Jay was setting a trap for himself: His attempt to avoid any similarity to his father was a statement of "Who I am not." The more relevant questions are, "Who are you?" and "What will you do to resolve your anger, fear, and disappointment?"

Motivation	And	Perception
Jay seeks safety (Level II) and comfort (Level III) needs for affiliation in the face of confrontation. It is important to his self-image (Level IV Psychological needs) to NOT react like his father during marital and other difficulties.	**WHAT** Significant Life Events * **SO WHAT** Lessons Learned * **NOW WHAT** How I show up in the current event	Jay has constructed a variety of "bad theories" around the use of strong emotions. He also confuses the difference between feeling anger (passion) Vs. acting out in a violent and abusive manner (abuses). He over-uses silence as a way to hide.

Figure 11

Up to this point, Jay not only buried painful memories, he also missed opportunities to be a leader in his family and at work as well as dismissing natural conflict-resolution survival tools to protect and nourish his self. It was as if he were wounded by the emotional shrapnel that resulted from the parental explosions.

"You are correct, Jay," I told him. "You should not smash your fist through a door or scream demeaning verbal obscenities at a loved one when you're upset. However, there's an important line between passion and abuse. I challenge you to find effective ways to express your emotions without reverting to violent and abusive behavior. I hope that you will learn from the past, not be silenced by it! Your father would wish the same for you. You could help erase the 'sins of the father' by becoming the man he hoped he could have been."

"Have you ever seen anyone like me and my family before?," Jay asked me.

"Absolutely," I acknowledged. "Most of us are so busy keeping secrets about the craziness that goes on in our families that we fail to learn the truth. Good people, like your father, often do DUM things. (See Chapter 10.) Secrets lose their power when they're no longer secrets. And people rarely change unless someone cares enough to 'care-front' them."

"But I'm embarrassed and ashamed," Jay said. "Why?," I asked him. "You were just a kid. You didn't do anything. I worry more that you get upset about the idea that you might blow your top whenever you allow yourself to feel anger or other appropriate emotions." Again, actions are different from emotions. We are **responsible** for our actions, but not for our emotions. The courts would be overflowing with poor souls like me (and maybe you!), who had momentary urges in extreme situations to cross the line and react with a vengeance.

Adults need to fight fair, rather than, as Jay did, not fight at all. Jay's dad certainly crossed the line. It is what he did with his anger that made him culpable. "I'd like to know more about your dad's lifeline to understand how he justifies his hot reactions. I don't believe that he intended to harm his family. I think his brain fell out. The interesting thing is that he probably felt like a victim. I believe you love him. But unless you resolve your negative emotions, I worry that you will only love each other at arm's length."

Jay surprised and impressed me when he said, "Okay. Let's do it. What would you suggest?"

What follows is a series of strategic steps that I advised Jay to use to engage in potentially heated conversations. The goal is to dismantle any barriers that might interfere with a frank, open, caring conversation—in this case, with his father.

Strategic Steps in "Care-Frontation"

Step 1. The first step is to clearly state the reasons for speaking up. "Dad, I love you. And I want to make sure that you don't misinterpret what I'm about to share. For years I've remained silent about certain of your words and actions when you get upset with Mom. When you react so strongly, it causes me to think of you in this way, which puts you in a bad light in my eyes. I'm not offering any threats or demands; I'm just asking you to listen to my concerns."

Step 2. Ask for clarity and intent. "I've seen and heard things between you and Mom that concern me. I need your help to understand what you mean when you say such hurtful things."

Step 3. Share your perspective. "I believe that you and Mom love each other. Otherwise, why do you stay together? I'm trying to understand how you escalate to the point of such harsh words and disheartening threats."

Step 4. Don't judge or interpret; just *listen* for understanding. Use Stephen Covey's Fifth Habit: "Seek first to understand; then to be understood."

Step 5. Repeat back what you've heard so that you can validate the person's thoughts and feelings. Remember, don't interpret or react, just listen for understanding!

Step 6. Maneuver among content, feelings and identity. Learn to maneuver among the three embedded dialogues in every difficult conversation (see Figure 12).

According to research by Stone, Patton, and Heen, difficult conversations are actually three separate and distinct dialogues:

Difficult Conversations
CONTENT Conversations—Explore what happened—the "facts", data, and each individual's perceptions of an event.
FEELINGS Conversations—Investigate how each person feels
IDENTITY Conversations—Seek to understand how the interaction impacts each participant.

Figure 12.

No matter what the subject, our thoughts and feelings fall into the same three categories:

Content. In most difficult conversations, individuals struggle to drive their perspective and make their points: Who is right, who meant what, and who is to blame. Content conversations typically drive people further apart, rather than to build consensus and improve relationships.

Feelings. Why? Because difficult conversations trigger strong emotions which, until they are effectively stated, understood, and managed, tend to further cloud situations and draw battle lines.

Identity. Conversations look inward toward the Self. How does what happened impact my self-esteem and self-confidence? Does the interaction build trust and affiliation or does it produce tension and defensive attitudes?

Let me offer an example of how these strategies work. The responses in **BOLD CAP ITALIC** type did not occur; they are meant as alternative ways to avoid the tension produced by the content-laden conversation (things that John **COULD HAVE SAID** to defuse the situation).

ACT I

John Upsets Mary—A Family Psychodrama:

John agreed to pick up Mary outside of work at 6 p.m. It is 6:20 p.m. when the harried husband arrives. It is dark and isolated ... and Mary is upset:

Mary: "You're late *as usual!* I can *never* depend on you!"

John: "I'm rarely late. Name one time that I've been late this month."

("YOU'RE RIGHT. WOW, I'M TWENTY MINUTES LATE. MY BOSS GRABBED ME ON THE WAY OUT. BUT THAT'S NOT AN EXCUSE. I'M SO SORRY IF I UPSET YOU.")

This type of response may have ended the argument. Please note: recognizing someone's feelings and taking responsibility for your contribution to the situation is not an admission of guilt. John did not do anything bad, but his being late did upset his partner. By the way, as the conflict escalates, John misses the opportunity to honor Mary's primary "identity-based" message:

"I don't feel like I matter to you, John. Work seems to be more important to you than me!"

Back to the drama— ACT II:

Mary: "Leave me alone. I've been waiting nearly an hour."

John: "You exaggerate. I'm not even a half-hour late. You ought to learn how to tell time." *("IT IS A LONG TIME TO WAIT. AND IT'S DARK AND ISOLATED HERE TOO. I'M SO SORRY. IT UPSETS ME WHEN YOU FEEL ANXIOUS.")*

Mary: (Silence)

John: "What do you think I was doing? Playing golf? I was at work!

Mary: (More silence accompanied by "the look" of disgust.)

John: "Well, for your information, I was with my boss. She asked me to explain charts for our upcoming meeting. What was I supposed to do, say I had to leave?"

Mary: "Work is always number one. I could freeze to death waiting for you."

John: "You exaggerate. What's the use of trying to talk to you."

Mary: (More silence ...)

This is a classic tit-for-tat "Content" discourse that escalates into a major blow-up. Both individuals are feeling misunderstood. Neither did anything wrong. John might have been better advised to avoid the content-level debate around "who is right", and not be drawn in by his wife's accusations. To repeat, he is **not** admitting any wrongdoing if he acknowledges Mary's emotions. The openings toward resolution are in Mary's primary messages: "I was frightened," (Emotions-level conversation) and "I sometimes feel as if I'm not important to you" (Identity-level conversation).

Jay's Conversation

Jay and I spent a great deal of time getting him ready for his meeting with his dad. He said that he felt like a gladiator preparing to meet a lion in the arena. I sensed his anxiety, especially in light of the painful history of his fear and unexpressed anger. It was important for him to remember that although he was struggling with memories from his childhood, he was no longer a child. Jay was going into the "arena" as a mature adult.

Jay not only survived in the "arena-of-emotions", he prospered as a result of the experience. He chose a very powerful strategy to engage his dad, one filled with respect and understanding. He decided *not* to ask his dad about his intentions behind his perceived overreactions. He chose instead to speak about himself and how he had learned to hide his emotions in silence. By doing so, he shared how he had to make major trade-offs for his silence and passivity, some which negatively impacted his ability to establish mature relationships. "I tried never to lie, Dad. But I often did not speak the emotional truth."

Jay confided in me that he rehearsed his introductory comments "a million times." What surprised him and made the event a positive marker experience for him was that his father voiced deep appreciation for the risk his son was taking. He simply cried when Jay told him of his horror at the top of the stairs. Jay expected his father to become defensive and resistant when he confessed that there were times when he did not like his father, "I always loved you, but there were times that I stopped liking you." His dad seemed to understand and asked Jay if he could ever forgive him. The two men began a dialogue, one that I will now reserve for father and son.

Difficult conversations succeed better when they are learning conversations where participants utilize Covey's "5th Habit," seeking first to understand, then to be understood.

When Jay later approached his mother with the same confession about his feelings for his father and the impact their arguments had on him, she reacted with the question, "Are you mad at me?" After that, she cried and apologized. No matter how hard he tried, his mother seemed to gradually retreat behind fortified walls of silence. It was at that moment that Jay had a major insight as to the frustration his father experienced when talking with his wife ... no shame, blame or judgments about her behavior, simply an admission by Jay that he was frustrated and confused as to how to proceed with any meaningful discussion when she took all blame yet retreated into silence.

I was especially proud of Jay when he shared an overview of his lifeline, including the explosive family episodes, during a later team-building session with his regional associates. He described how his colleagues reached out to each other to tell him of their painful stories and uncovered the painful remnants of years gone by that they had swept beneath their "carpets."

Jay seemed genuinely surprised and troubled by the misperceptions he faced with his team members. They confessed to Jay that his passivity caused them to hold back any feedback. They believed that Jay did not give a damn about what people thought about him or about how they felt. His regional manager confessed that he had recommended that Jay be passed over for promotion because he was convinced that Jay lacked the passion and sense of ownership to align with the company's cultural values.

One piece of feedback seemed especially important to Jay. A co-worker said, "I can identify with you. I used to believe that when I held back and did not give honest feedback it was because I did not want to hurt the other person's feelings. That's not true. I didn't give honest feedback because I did not want to feel uncomfortable. I was selfishly thinking about me, not the other person."

Parroting Is Not Communicating

I also believe that Jay's previous silence was a missed opportunity to act as a leader in his family, as well as at work during volatile situations.

Silence is also an ineffective listening strategy. Some individuals insist that silence is needed in order to absorb the content of the speaker's message. They therefore define listening as being able to capture and repeat back what a speaker says. Parrots can do that too. Communication is meant to be a loop ... listen *and* respond.

Effective listening requires some form of verbal and non-verbal responses, e.g., a simple, "I see what you mean; that makes sense," or a non-verbal nod or thumbs-up hand gesture to denote agreement. Otherwise, silence, can create ambiguity --- "He didn't say anything; I had a sense that he may not have agreed with what I was saying. I wonder what he was really feeling and thinking?"

Epilogue on Jay

Jay occasionally sent me updates about the conversations he continued to have with both his father and mother. I felt especially happy when he wrote, "We are becoming a healthy family; Dad lost his negative voice and Mom found her voice." I smiled when he said, "Mom's gone from a silent victim to one tough cookie; Dad and I hesitate to mess with her."

I wrote him a final note thanking him for being so patient and open during our coaching sessions, as well as for the happy ending.

"Jay," I wrote him back, "you remind me of Don Quixote, the mythical 'Man of La Mancha'. He too set out on a quest for the ultimate truth. On his journey he discovered something that may prove useful to you and your family:

Don't confuse the <u>facts</u> with the <u>truth</u>.

Don Quixote's wisdom might be especially valuable to you in the relationship you are pursuing with your own parents. When you and important people from your past reflect back to earlier events, the "facts" may seem quite clear. Please consider this: troubling facts often hide deeper truths.

<u>MAP</u> each other's behavior and you may see beyond the wounds of the past into the heart of the matter.

CHAPTER 13

I Am A Rock

"I Am A Rock"
P. Simon, 1965

A winter's day
In a deep and dark December
I am alone
Gazing from my window
To the streets below
On a freshly fallen silent shroud of snow
I am a rock
I am an island
I've built walls
A fortress deep and mighty
That none may penetrate
I have no need of friendship
Friendship causes pain
It's laughter and it's loving I disdain
I am a rock
I am an island
Don't talk of love
Well I've heard the word before
It's sleeping in my memory
I won't disturb the slumber
Of feelings that have died
If I never loved I never would have cried
I am a rock
I am an island
I have my books
And my poetry to protect me
I am shielded in my armor
Hiding in my room
Safe within my womb
I touch no one and no one touches me
I am a rock
I am an island
And a rock feels no pain.
And an island never cries.

Feeling No Pain?

"The Sound of Silence" is the chart-topping album that propelled the 1960s folk-rock music duo Simon and Garfunkel to popularity. Among the songs in the album is one titled "I Am A Rock" which contains lyrics about remaining emotionally isolated and purposely maintaining that detachment as a way of coping.

The lyrics of the song send a complex message regarding the mixed signals surrounding keeping an emotional distance from others. The words "I am a rock" in the song might help explain the "strength" of never complaining or remaining strong under fire, perhaps, but it's the second part of the refrain that concerns me ... "I am an island." It's the loneliness and missed opportunities we face when we set ourselves apart as an island, when we "build walls," "have no need of friendship," as the song says, and we observe events rather than actively pursuing a spirited partnership with others.

"I Am A Rock" also describes a recurring theme in the life of an incredible women who I had the privilege of meeting as a result of her bout with cancer. At the time, my wife (a cancer survivor herself) and I were offering open sessions on Wednesday evenings for individuals who wanted to share feelings about their cancer. After these support-group discussions, I would lead various forms of deep relaxation as a tool to manage the mental and physical discomfort that accompanied treatment of what I call the *"dis-ease."*

The woman to whom I referred, Cece (not her real name, see Foreword), was in her early forties and told the group that she had always imagined that she would get cancer. This way of thinking began when, at the age of seventeen, she was misdiagnosed by a physician. She was told that a benign fatty cyst in her left breast was cancerous. The doctor recommended immediate surgery and warned Cece's mother that the child might have to face the possibility of a radical mastectomy. Cece said that she kept mentally repeating what she called her "death mantra"—"I am damaged goods." She continued to repeat this thought process even after the diagnosis was corrected and non-surgically treated. Even though Cece had no surgical scars, she imagined herself disfigured, and felt sure that no man would ever want her.

Although everything pointed to a full recovery, Cece said she never felt safe from that day forward. "It was as if I was mentally rehearsing for a catastrophic event to befall me," she recounted. "I imagined all kinds of horror stories as to how I would react to the trauma. The irony is, now that it's here, [an actual cancer diagnosis] I'm handling it."

An Island of Unspoken Feelings

During a series of one-on-one sessions, I had the opportunity to <u>MAP</u> (Motivation And Perception) Cece's lifeline. One of the many blessings in her life was her father, who was devoted to his family. Cece had a very special bond with her dad. The one regret she had was that they never spoke on a feelings level with him, however. She described how her father would change the subject if anyone in the family was upset. "He never wanted to hear bad news," she explained. "He would give you a hug and say, 'Don't worry, it'll pass.'"

Before she began her life-story, I spoke with Cece. "I appreciate that you're sharing your father's choice to remain silent regarding how he felt," I told her. "But what did he say to you as a child when you told him that you wanted to share your feelings with him? Did he yell? Walk out of the room? Take away your privileges?" I suspected the answer, but hoped she would understand the intent of my questions.

"I never told him," Cece answered, as I expected she would. "Why?," I asked her. "It was important to you." "I guess that I did not want to make him uncomfortable," she responded.

Cece then shared her most special moments with her dad. She recalled how she would go to bed after completing an important school project — like the time she attempted to make a model of St. Basil's Cathedral from egg cartons and cardboard boxes — and her dad tucked her in and gave her his special hug, ending the day with his trademark remark, "Oh, did I tell you that I still love you? And I always will." She's not sure if she just imagined it … or not, but the words, "And I always will …." seemed to guide her gently into sweet dreams.

Then, when Cece awoke, it was as if a good fairy had visited. In this case, something had changed with her project … a touch of paint here, a shaved steeple there, little, helpful touches that made her project just a little bit better. Cece felt as if a special guardian angel was watching out for her.

I could not help but ask her how her dad responded when she thanked him for his helpful deeds. She seemed surprised that I asked, however.

"I never said anything," she said. Nor did her dad. These two wonderful people were acting in collusions of silence.

About the Good Stuff

As you may recall from personal revelations made earlier, after the age of four, I never had a father, so what I'm about to say (with the best of intentions) comes from a place of hope, but—quite frankly—jealousy as well. It is a great mystery to me why children do not tell their fathers and other closest loved ones (moms, brothers, sisters, etc.) that they love them, and express to them what I call "the good stuff". I understand why grown children might not drag up the pain and drama from the past ... like when Jay's dad broke the front door and stormed off into the night, but I do not understand why the "good stuff" of the past is not acknowledged.

What's at risk if you do share the special, loving memories? And what's at risk if you don't? At the risk of sounding morbid, please don't save precious messages to a loved one for the Emergency Room when he may be in route to the final resting place.

Connect the Dots

When Cece and I began to connect the dots, she initially forgot to mention that her father was a World War II veteran who had experienced the unspeakable in the Pacific. I understand why he did not speak of the war; soldiers will only do that with other soldiers. "You had to be there to understand," might be the underlying rationale for silence in theaters of war.

As it turned out, Cece had been three years old when her father left for the war, and nearly six years old when he returned. What happened when she first saw her Dad walk in the door after nearly a three-year absence? Cece had only faint recollections of the arrival of a tall, handsome soldier running over and grabbing her mother. She remembers being frightened by it. "Mom screamed and cried. I thought he was hurting her," she explained. "I ran and hid."

That was all she remembered, and nothing was explained to her at the time. Over the years, still there was no family discussion or collective consciousness of the reunion. It was as if her dad had simply returned from a short business trip.

It is important to me that you do not hear any criticism or finger pointing in my description of events or in my questioning of Cece. Digging into her childhood was necessary, as this same type of behavior continued to show up in Cece's life, behavior that ultimately did not serve her well personally or professionally.

Loving, But Silent?

Cece eventually mimicked the loving but silent traditions of her father. For example, she made it a quiet habit to slip notes and cards into her husband's suitcase when he went on business trips. She was also always present in the audience and athletic stands to witness her children's events — always there for them, if not outwardly expressing how she felt about them. "I want them to know that I am here for them," she said simply.

Dr. Joe Currier

I was very impressed with her dedication and quiet love for her family — no brag, just action. Those are the admirable points. The "at risk" points arose when Cece told me that her husband occasionally questioned her passion for him. He once accused her of doing what pleased *her*, not *him*. He appreciated the notes and cards, but wanted words and hugs when he came home from his business trips, for example. And, it was not clear if her children may had begun to feel some of the same way.

First, I told Cece how much I admired her, but that I wondered why she did not celebrate the "Power of **and**" — quietly marking events with a card **and** physically show up in the moment!

Eventually, our coaching relationship with Cece ended, but years later she wrote me a note. She gave me permission to share it:

I woke from a sound sleep the evening following our last session. I recalled a dream. In it, my dad was sitting alone in the backyard. I tried to speak to him, but no words came out of my mouth. Dad seemed sad … as if he needed my help. This is where the dream ended. I woke my husband and told him to pack an overnight bag. I needed to go home. It must have been the look in my eyes that told him that I was going with or without him and the children.

It was 3 a.m. when we pulled out of our driveway. We arrived at 6:00 a.m. and just sat napping in front of my parents home until Dad, coming out to get the morning paper, tapped on the car window. "Are you okay?," he asked. "What's wrong?" I got out of the car and assured him that everything was fine.

"Dad I need to take a walk with you." I said. "It's important that you know something. I am so ashamed of myself that I never told you how much it meant to me to know that you were watching over me all my life." I gave him a long list of examples of his nightly visits.

"My dad tried to emotionally deflect by saying, 'I'm your father; that's my job.' Warm, loving gestures always seemed to be difficult for him to receive. I now wonder if it was that he never thought he had earned my love and respect. And it did not help that I never told him the impact he has had on me!"

"But those days are gone. I was not going to let him off with a safe deflection. I told him my truths and shared my deep love and respect for him."

"WE CRIED. **AND** FOR THE NEXT FOUR YEARS WE NEVER MISSED ANOTHER OPPORTUNITY TO SHOW UP FOR EACH OTHER."

"He was in a coma for nearly a month before he died. I broke the silence with my words and gentle touch … I wanted him to know that this little fairy was keeping watch over him."

"I appreciate the years we had after I broke the silence. I would hate to think that he might have gone without knowing the impact he had on me."

Guess What?

"I had the best father on the planet ... and he knows it ... ***Because I told him!***"

It's your turn.

CHAPTER 14

What's At Risk . . . If I Change?

"When you arrive at the fork in the road,
TAKE IT."

--Yogi Berra

W-A-R

Let's play a game called W-A-R, a coaching methodology that explores the impact of one's choices on self and others ... What's-At-Risk if I behave one way versus another? We will get to this methodology in a bit, but let's first introduce a manager in need of this.

Ellen (not her real name, see Foreword), a mid-level manager in a *Fortune 500* sales organization, struggled with this question when she kept refusing job promotions. For over five years, senior managers had been asking her to lead various teams. They knew that she was a star-performer, which meant that she had both character and competency. The only thing that held her back was her inability to hold people accountable.

When Ellen was given stretch-assignments as a preview to what it would be like to serve as a team leader, she always delivered a quality product on time, but in the process she allowed people who reported to her to delay assignments and lower their standards of excellence. When I say that she allowed this, I do not mean that she condoned these behaviors. In fact, these behaviors upset her deeply. She considered their actions and omissions were unacceptable. However, instead of confronting the problems face-to-face with the individuals involved, she corrected the errors and completed the tasks herself.

Ellen was upset with the individuals who dropped the ball, and angry at herself for not saying anything to them. She believed that the answer to her managerial dilemma was to find better ways to motivate her direct reports. When she sought the advice of a senior associate, he agreed that it was important to motivate the employees; that was a leadership opportunity. He also told her that the job of a manager was to provide fair, firm, timely consequences for each individual's actions.

"It's important to recognize and reward positive outcomes," he told her. "And you must hold people accountable when they fail to meet the agreed upon standards and deadlines."

Ellen recalled his *"A-B-C FORMULA"* to become a successful manager:

Antecedents—Behavior—Consequences

The "A" in the formula, Antecedents are the things a manager does *before* an event. This means that managers teach, advise, coach, and encourage members of a team. They also must establish clear expectations and create verbal agreements and presumptions related to who does what, when, where and how.

The "B" is a reminder that *Behavior* generally should improve over time. How often is it said, "Wow, if I knew then what I know now, I would have done even better!"? This refers to the fact that people naturally learn from their experiences, which means that a manager who provides feedback enables the individual to understand what needs improvement, which then translates into better performance outcomes. At least that is how things are supposed to evolve. Individuals do not always do the right thing regardless of how much time, teaching, and opportunities for practice are provided.

The "C" refers to the *Consequences* of the choices made, both positive and negative. When people are praised and materially rewarded for their actions, they tend to repeat those behaviors. Recognition and rewards often motivate people to perform to an ever-improving standard. However, individuals also have the option of falling on bad habits, making excuses for not fulfilling our promises or living up to our agreements. A manager needs to provide feedback and negative consequences for poor behavior and performance as well.

Holding People Accountable

Ellen understood the concept of the "carrot and the stick." Although she was comfortable with the "carrot"—the idea of rewarding people for effective, on-time behavior, it was the "stick" that troubled her. She found it difficult to confront and hold people accountable for their negative behavior. When Ellen discussed this perplexing situation, she grimaced signaling sadness and pain, and overall resistance to the responsibility of holding people accountable for the things that they agreed to do.

It was at this point that I suggested that she needed to realize that the manager is not being a villain in holding direct reports responsible for their failures to perform up to par, but just being responsible. The rewards and punishments are embedded in the performance contract. A manager's responsibility is to clearly define, monitor, and administrate the contract. This is not a rationalization to avoid responsibility for delivering consequences.

The point I am making is that individuals' *choices* determine their outcome. As an effective manager, I need to be willing to do whatever is reasonable within my powers to help my partners to succeed. It would be irresponsible of me to not hold them culpable for their actions. That outcome would not only keep the individuals in the purgatory of underachieving, it would also undermine the efforts of other team members who *are* completing their responsibilities. My inaction could also encourage bad personal habits, thereby breeding additional failure to achieve and create lower self-confidence and esteem for the underachievers.

Ellen intellectually agreed with everything I suggested, but worried that people would think she was mean if she held her direct reports accountable for their underperformance. I told her that she was operating under a faulty assumption, namely, that holding people accountable for their own behavior is cruel. I believed that Ellen was making excuses to hide the fact that care-frontation made her feel personally uncomfortable, and I sought to find out why. She agreed to <u>MAP</u> her behavior.

What ... So What ... Now What

Ellen is a staff accountant who has been considered for promotion to a management position on several occasions. Everyone agrees that she is the most qualified person for the job. However, her hesitation to hold people accountable for work delays and shoddy products has held her back.

Looking at her behavior in view of Maslow's Hierarchy of Human Needs (see Chapter 6), Ellen seeks a secure work environment (Level II safety need) and comfort (Level III social need). It is important to her self-image (a Level IV psychological need for acceptance) to avoid confrontation at all costs.

Motivation	And	Perception
Ellen seeks safety (Level II) and comfort (Level III need for Affiliation) in the face of confrontation. It is important to her self-image (Level IV Psychological needs) to never play a "villain" role in family or work dramas. Her solution is to just be quiet and do it herself.	**WHAT** Significant Life Events * **SO WHAT** Lessons Learned * **NOW WHAT** How I show up in the current event	Ellen has constructed "bad theories" to justify her avoidance behavior. She equates confrontation to abandonment. "When people get angry, someone always departs." Therefore, "fighting is bad."

Connect the Dots

Ellen began discussing her life-story by confiding in me that she kept a lot of secrets. For one thing, although she wanted to be promoted, she confided that she suspected that she was making excuses about being non-confrontational. She further admitted that she felt very angry when she cleaned up the messes that other people made. But, despite her strong feelings about her desire to change her behavior, she continued to complete other people's tasks and avoided confronting those who were simply not doing the right thing.

Dr. Joe Currier

"I chose to suffer in silence rather than be a bad guy," she told me. Working alone is an avoidance behavior she used. "I don't like to push people. I'm afraid they'll be upset, which troubles me," she said. "I'd rather just do things myself than to go through the hassle of pushing and pulling people to do things they do not want to do. If they wanted to do it, they would not have to be monitored."

The next secret required my professional assurance that I would not breach her confidence. No one in Ellen's office knew that her parents were divorced. She avoided talking about her family and shared nothing more than that she is an only child. That is technically not true. Ellen simply does not finish the sentence, which would be, "I am an only child of this marriage." Her dad had two additional children after the divorce.

The faulty assumptions that stifled Ellen's power to express her authentic self[12] grew out of a downward spiraling psychodrama that she witnessed as a child. Her mom always seemed to be displeased by Ellen's dad's lack of ambition. For as long as Ellen could recall, her mother would maliciously accuse her father of being lazy. Her mother would taunt her father with the accusation, "A real man would be a better provider."

Ellen's dad enjoyed the challenge of being a field engineer. He had no desire to manage people; to do so would require him to work in a stuffy office and to wear what he referred to as a monkey suit, a formality he left behind when he retired from the United States Army. Her dad met and married her mom, a native of Berlin, while serving on active duty in Germany. After he was honorably discharged, the family put down roots in Cincinnati.

It was not long until her dad realized that his wife expected what he referred to as a "country club" lifestyle, something that he was not interested in. Ellen spoke with pride when she described her dad as "a simple man with simple needs." Her dad made a salary that afforded the family a comfortable lifestyle, and he was troubled that he could never satisfy his wife. At first he tolerated his wife's negative remarks because he suspected that they were the result of her struggling with personal memories of the aftermath of WWII and the nightmarish recollections her family suffered under the Third Reich and in the aftermath of the bombings. He had hoped that her dissatisfaction would eventually pass.

Her dad chose to remain quiet whenever her mom ranted and raved. Ellen believed that he did so in an effort to protect her. The nightly ritual of name-calling intensified as the years passed. Ellen's recollections were, "Mom would

---

12   For more information, see Glossary of Terms and Text References at back.

yell. Dad would just wink at me and ask me to go to my room. At some point, Mom would storm up the stairs and Dad would end up downstairs in the basement alone."

Ellen's theories evolved to include myths like "fighting is bad." That made sense during her childhood. In her life, when her parents fought, "someone ended up sleeping on the couch, and eventually went out the door." The latter part of her troubling false-belief happened when she was in high school when her dad left and eventually remarried.

It did not take me long to conclude that Ellen's primary challenge was to figure out what to do with her power. She had a personal presence and passion that shouted, "I'm ready to rock!" She was a very assertive, outgoing woman. Her persona changed when she partnered with people who were not self-motivated; she repressed her anger in fear that she might **over**-react like her mother. Instead, she **under**-reacted.

It upset her when I asked if she worried that she might have the driving spirit of her mother. I had to clarify that I was not referring to her mom's negativity and abusive behavior, but desire for success. My opinion was that instead of figuring how to better express her passionate nature, Ellen neutered herself with excuses.

This is how the W-A-R game went:

What's At Risk IF I Assert Myself	What's At Risk IF I Do NOT Assert Myself
People might think I'm kissing up to the bosses.	My bosses and peers may think I'm kissing up to my direct reports.
Peers and direct reports might get upset with me and not talk to me. They may not want me to lead them.	My bosses might get upset and give up on me as if I'm a hopeless case. They might not consider me for further promotion.
People might talk behind my back and say I'm mean.	Bosses might talk behind my back and say I'm weak and ineffective
People might verbally attack me, "Who do you think you are? We thought we were friends."	Bosses might verbally attack me, "What's wrong with you? You're letting us down."

Notice that the reactions are similar no matter what she does, and the possible threats are the same. The difference is that the outcome changes. If she does not assert herself, Ellen runs the risk of living in the shadow of fear and not receiving the recognition and opportunities she desires and deserves. If she

Dr. Joe Currier

does assert herself, however, the outcome is likely to change. She will probably be promoted and, therefore, make herself and her family proud.

I suggested that the real risk was in the "If I Fail to Assert Myself" sequence; she loses in a variety of ways if she **chooses** to hide in the bad assumptions from the past. Negative reactions in the "If I Assert Myself" sequence are *possible,* but she can manage these reactions if they arise by learning how to resolve tension and to build loyal, efficient, and effective teams.

The flipside of the scenario is a personal and career trap. If Ellen does not assert herself, she will *probably* suffer consequences that do not belong to her; they belong to her direct reports. It becomes a lose-lose equation. Her direct reports do not receive the care-frontation that could get them out of their poor performance rut **and** Ellen remains behind as others climb the career ladder right past her.

Ellen is not alone in her W-A-R drama. There are many other men and women who are heading into self-defeating career dead ends. They are scripted to replay a familiar psychodrama by acting on faulty assumptions and false theories.

New life <u>MAP</u>s are within reach ... but there is a price:

It will NOT BE COMFORTABLE.
It requires a NEW MINDSET.
It's a matter of CHOICE.

CHAPTER 15

What Did the Empathetic Surgeon Do?

Question:
"What Did the
Empathetic Surgeon Do?"

The Empathetic Surgeon?

Let's consider the title question:

"What did the empathetic surgeon do?"

Answer: "Nothing!"

Outcome? The patient died!

So, what would the answer to the question be, and how would the outcome change, if we replaced the word "surgeon" with your primary roles at work and at home?

What did the empathetic *manager* do when she learned that an employee lied about going on a sales call? Nothing! She knew that he did not go on the sales call but, because his sales numbers sucked she felt sorry for him. "I wanted to cut him some slack." And what was the outcome? Neither the manager nor the salesman benefited. The manager was passed over for a promotion and assigned to a different area, and a new manager came on board and fired the salesman.

"What did the empathetic *wife* do when her husband repeatedly got out of control and verbally abused her?" Again, nothing! She justified his behavior: "He's a very passionate person ... He doesn't mean to hurt me?" And what is the outcome? Again, a dead end.

"What did the empathetic *father* do after excessively punishing, and abusing his young son, Johnny?" The answer is, yet again, nothing! At 8 p.m. on Tuesday evening, he went into his child's room and apologized for his over-reaction at the dinner table when Johnny spilled the milk. He 'patiently' instructed his son on table etiquette. "You need to be more careful and pay attention. I'm sorry that I hurt your arm when I jerked you out of the chair and sent you to your room without dinner. I'm just trying to teach you, like my father taught me." What was the outcome?

And, then "What did that same empathetic father do at 8 p.m. on Wednesday evening?" The answer is he trudged into his child's room and apologized *again* for his overreaction when Johnny handed him his report card. He 'patiently' explained why he slapped him in the back of the head, called him a "dummy," and sent him to his room. "I'm only trying to teach you the value of a good education." And what was the outcome?

I encourage you to take it from here. You have the questions, the answers, and can predict the outcomes. Let me know what you decide about the next opportunity you face on the job and in your family.

Oh, and don't forget to ask the question, "How's your strategy working? How's that working for you?"

Excuses

EXCUSES

EXCUSES

If any one of these three words describes your response to a question above, it's time to connect the dots and <u>MAP</u> a new strategy.

Your current one may be a dead end.

CHAPTER 16

Who's On First?

Non-Responsive Answers?

"Who's on third base?"

"No, What's on third base. Who's on first."

"I don't know! That's why I'm asking!"

The above sequence is part of the "Who's on First?" comedy routine made famous by the 1940s comedy team Abbott and Costello. In the routine, Abbott identifies the players on a baseball team to Costello, but the players' names and nicknames -- such as "Who" and "I Don't Know"—can be interpreted as non-responsive answers to Costello's questions. (For anyone who has no idea of what I am referring to, I urge you to view a six-minute U-Tube clip of the routine, *http://www.youtube.com/watch?v=sShMA85pv8M.*)

The reason I bring up this comedy routine is that the seemingly non-responsiveness involved reminds me of a situation I encountered during a team-building workshop. It just so happens that a person I met during this workshop provided me with a great way to end this book.

Here's what happened — and please don't tell me there is no cosmic plan out there for each of us. This just whacked me up side my head! I was finishing what I thought was the final chapter when I met Max (not his real name, see Foreword), a high-potential middle manager, who faced a disturbing conundrum that I thought illustrated important key points I have shared throughout this book. I knew immediately that I needed, with his permission and promise of anonymity of course, to add a chapter about him to this book before coming to a close.

I met Max when a colleague of mine and I were facilitating a team-building workshop for a relatively small, yet elite professional organization. We went into the meeting challenged by the ambivalent feedback we received in a confidential survey from the attendees. There were mixed emotions on very primary levels among senior members of the organization.

A Leaderless Team?

For example, there was a great deal of resistance to our efforts to unite members as a team and even more tension around the idea of leadership. No one seemed to agree upon, or accept, who was in charge. When it came to a discussion of role responsibility, I felt as if I was trapped in the "Who's On First?" comedy routine! The simplest questions would produce silence and "puppy stares." When I asked the participants to write down whom they considered the current leader of the group, I received five different names out of a group of fifteen.

In desperation in trying to find a starting point, my partner and I decided to abandon efforts to build a team. Instead, we encouraged people to consider themselves as tenants-in-common in a newly formed neighborhood.

I quoted Scott Peck in his book "The Road Less Traveled":

> "The very real steps in building community come when someone speaks at a level of authenticity and vulnerability at which no one in the group has spoken before."

My associate and I then introduced an exercise that could help us move toward this communal goal. We asked about anything that people admired, appreciated, and valued in the organization and the people they worked with. We also recommended that they explore whatever caused them personal and professional pain. Then we asked what could be done to improve both performance and satisfaction?

Taking the "Open Seat"

Max, a mature seasoned professional, was the first to volunteer for the "open seat," which means that he settled into a high chair at the front of the room and introduced himself. Our objective was to help these "work-neighbors" in this newly defined community to get to better know each other and thereby build relationships that could serve them as they interacted and worked toward a variety of common goals. Max told his co-workers, who appeared shocked by his initiative, that he was willing to go outside of his comfort zone and explore some of the leadership principles we had shared in the morning session.

Max rocked the house! He took the opportunity to give not only the obligatory surface introduction of "name, rank, and serial number" so to speak. He spoke of marker events in his life that helped shape the individual he is today. Max mesmerized his work-neighbors with his recollection of years gone by.

It was especially painful, yet a privilege and blessing, when he shared his most devastating memory. At the age of eight, Max's father had committed suicide. He did not elaborate too much beyond that, other than to imply that it may have had some connection to a relationship that his mother had with his dad's business partner. I say "imply" because it was clear that Max never fully understood, nor sought to clarify, the situation. While he said he was curious about the circumstances surrounding his father's death, he also seemed even more disturbed by the rapid appearance and disappearance of different men who passed through the portals of his home-life following his dad's death. Max said he did not want to cause his mom any further pain by seeking closure to this family tragedy, so he remained silent.

As he "connected the dots" in his life, one of the recurring themes in Max's story was the hypercritical nature of his mother. "If I brought home a 98 on my report card, my mother would ask me what happened to the other two points," he recounted. "When I pitched a little league no-hitter, she criticized my not going four-for-four at bat. She never praised the fact that I hit the winning home run; instead, she scolded me for striking out in the third inning. She said that I let my teammates down. No matter what I did, it was never good enough!"

Max minimized the painful negative impact of these events by assuring the group that he believed his mother's intentions were good. "In my head I know that my mother only wanted the best for me. But in my heart, it always hurt." The constant barrage of negativity eventually caused Max to simply give up any hope of healthy recognition from his mom.

What he did not realize was that parts of his mother-son psychodrama gradually crept into his own behavior. For one thing, he hated any form of feedback; to him, feedback *felt* as if someone was mocking him. He confessed to his work-neighbors that his automatic default response to feedback was to shoot the person an angry look as if to say, "Mind your own business. If I want your opinion, I will ask for it!" Like his mother, he intended no harm; he was just trying to protect his severely bruised ego. What Max failed to realize was that his mindset (the negative, resentful self-talk) was masked by his hostile body language. People did not understand that he was protecting himself, but instead felt Max's anger and kept him at a safe emotional distance. When I asked him what he imagined when he received feedback and felt criticized by it, he said that it was as if he was a combination of a "stupid person" and a "naughty child" (Identity[13]).

Max's work-neighbors expressed surprise and appreciation for his sharing his life-story. They had misinterpreted his office behavior and apologized for socially isolating him. People knew that Max was uncomfortable with feedback, but falsely assumed that it was his ego that got in the way. Behind his back, people had been saying, "Don't waste your time talking with Max. He's arrogant and closed to feedback. He's a know-it-all."

Content. *In most difficult conversations, individuals struggle to drive their perspective and make their points: Who is right, who meant what, and who is to blame. Content conversations typically drive people further apart, rather than to build consensus and improve relationships.*

---

13   Max's thoughts and feelings, which related to "Identity," looked inward to the self. Consider concepts discussed in Chapter 12 about the three categories of communication: Content, Emotion, and Identity.

Dr. Joe Currier

Feelings. Why? Because difficult conversations trigger strong emotions which, until they are effectively stated, understood, and managed, tend to further cloud situations and draw battle lines.

Identity. Conversations look inward toward the Self. How does what happened impact my self-esteem and self-confidence? Does the interaction build trust and affiliation or does it produce tension and defensive attitudes?

Max recalled an office event that demonstrated the level of conflict he experienced. He recalled how Mary, his supervisor, had once offered him a suggestion regarding a shortcut to one of the annoying monthly reports everyone was expected to file. Max admitted that his self-talk refuted any possibility that the feedback was a sign of goodwill and support. The voice in his head shouted, "Shame on you. What's wrong with you? Mary thinks you're stupid!"

Mary, who was a part of this workshop, had personalized the event and told Max that she had assumed that he simply did not like her. "I was trying to be a good neighbor," she said. "I kept asking people if I came across like a know-it-all bitch. I'm so sorry."

Max and Mary attempted to build a collegial-bridge by engaging in a **Content**-level discussion. Both offered important cognitive-information around the event itself. When there was an appropriate opening in the discussion, I attempted to add Feelings and Identity levels of communication, which is where partnerships and level II and III relationships are formed, as you may recall from Chapters 3 and 12.

I asked Max, "How did you **feel** (Emotions) and what was the impact (Identity) of the interaction?" He was quick to admit feeling both angry and embarrassed. "I thought you were putting me down," he told Mary. "As if you thought I was stupid. It never dawned on me that you were trying to help me." When I asked Max, "Who's voice were you hearing: Mary's, yours, or Mom's?" He hesitated and then responded, "Mom's." There was a look of deep pain on his face.

Max was intrigued when two colleagues reported similar childhood parenting experiences and how these lowered their self-esteem. Up to this point, Max had believed that he was the problem and that his mom was just doing what good parents do. He always believed that he was a loser and resented feedback because it felt like others were rubbing his nose in his shortcomings.

MAP-ing Max's Behavior

The "What—So What—Now What" model was beginning to make sense. I feared that there was too much of a back-story to Max's family history and was concerned that we might cause more harm than good if we moved too quickly into the hidden agendas regarding his mom's behavior in relation to her marriage and events that led up to his dad's suicide.

I played it safe by asking the team to help Max to M-A-P a new life path, *if* he was open to their suggestions. Max seemed genuinely pleased that people would take such an interest in his life. He was reframing a recurring negative belief ("All feedback is a malicious attack on one's ego"). Instead of labeling the feedback as character assassination and cheap put-downs, he appreciated how people were willing to help by sharing their life experiences and perceptions.

I was banking on the fact that Max would recall something that we explored earlier in the day, "feedback is just information" —not criticism—and that only one human being on the planet gets to decide if the information is accurate and of value in relation to his future choices. That one person is "me"—in this case Max. Our obligation as peer-partners, or work-neighbors in this process, is to share our perceptions in a non-judgmental, caring manner. It is Max's responsibility to cull through the data and utilize any valuable feedback.

Motivation	And	Perception
Max had been on a mission to please his mother, a task that although virtually impossible to achieve over the years, he continued to pursue, despite causing himself inner turmoil and social pressure. His failure to find safety, acceptance, recognition and approval, caused him to over- or under-react to any form of feedback.	**WHAT** Significant Life Events * **SO WHAT** Lessons Learned * **NOW WHAT** How I show up in the current event	Max had built a series of "self-defeating theories", e.g., "All feedback is bad!", which caused him to be estranged from his peer-partners. Any feedback, no matter how well intentioned, was ignored, challenged or simply "blown off."

Max's life journey had repeatedly been hijacked by powerful marker events that he did not fully understand. How could he? Max was an innocent child in a dysfunctional adult world. By the way, when I explained this to Max, he did not agree and tried to protect his mother. I apologized, adding, "Max, I'm offering you data. I am sorry if you hear me judging or demonizing your mother. I am not. I believe that she was doing the best she could at the time."

I was not willing to leave it there. Max is a parent himself now. He is the father of three children, a son and two daughters. I wish you could have seen his face when I suggested that he place one of his children in a scenario similar to the one he experienced. "Which of your three children would you have grow up like you did?" I asked him. He responded immediately, "Are you crazy?!" With that protective parental mindset, I believe that Max, perhaps for the first time in his life, began to understand the trauma he had experienced.

It never ceases to amaze me how survivors do not recognize the pure insanity and pain of having grown up in a dysfunctional world—that is, until someone suggests placing a loved one who is under their protection into such an impossible, demeaning, ego-destructive environment.

It became clear to me and to Max's peer-partners that there were continual landmines all along Max's life highway. It's no wonder that he developed a victim's mentality. It was not safe for him to challenge his mom. It was easier to channel that energy into interpersonal theories that allowed him to assert himself. His silence and hostile body language was a passive-aggressive "screw you" to anyone who he imagined was calling him a loser. The problem was, no one was calling him a "loser." At worst, people were challenging or questioning his *behavior*, not his person.

Max seemed very pleased after he opened up to the group. He felt understood and respected. He also reported that he valued this type of team-building experience and hoped that people would take advantage of the "open seat" and bring this straight talk, care-frontation methodology into the office.

Developmental Feedback or Déjà vu?

This was just the quiet before the storm. Everything that happened up to this point is not the reason I decided to add this chapter. It's what happened next that I believe will be of greater value.

We continued the workshop into the evening and ended the day with a celebratory dinner. We had a second half-day session during which many colleagues sat in the open seat, having been inspired by Max's courage to do so. Each person took the opportunity to share important parts of his or her own life story. The work-neighbors, or members of this new community, were beginning to establish meaningful bonds that could serve them well personally and professionally.

In Conclusion, Jumping to Conclusions

At the end of the meeting, I offered participants the opportunity to close the experience with parting words of appreciation to anyone in the group who may have positively impacted them.

I was surprised when Max interrupted with an alarming warning. He appeared visibly shaken. "I'm so disappointed," he said. "I thought this stuff was the real deal, but it's not." He stood up and was about to walk out in a huff, but said he first wanted to caution his colleagues about my associate and me, claiming we had set a dangerous trap. "This is psychobabble that promises eternal bliss if we just love our neighbors," he said. "But there's a catch. You'd better do it *their* way or else!"

This abrupt declaration stopped the closing process in its tracks. None of us knew what had happened to make Max say these things, but he came across loud and clear. I still could not figure out why he felt the way he did, and decided to ask him. I also wanted to turn this event into a teaching opportunity, so I paused. I was afraid that my actions might be perceived as either disrespectful or defensive (Intention vs. Impact), both of which would not serve Max or the emerging community.

When I told Max that I could see that he was upset and asked him to clarify why, he answered by verbally attacking my co-facilitator, who had spoken to him privately, offering some constructive suggestions about his speaking habits. This became an issue with Max, as he fell back into old habits of being upset about feedback in any form.

Oh, and did I mention that my co-facilitator for the workshop is a woman? Max felt that she (my associate) had just ambushed him in the hallway during the break. "Your side-kick criticized the way I talk," he announced. "She said that I over-used the phrase, 'You know,' while I was telling my story. Who the hell is she to criticize me?!" Max raised his voice and seemed especially insulted by the fact that my associate was "keeping score." "She had the nerve to tell me that I repeated the phrase twenty-three times!"

Max continued with his outrage, "I can't believe the insensitivity and disrespect I just experienced!" he said. "I'm out of here." He repeated the threat, but still did not move toward the door. It seemed obvious to me that an ill-timed coaching opportunity by my associate triggered a default response Max had learned over the many years of harsh maternal disapproval. He heard, "It's never good enough, dummy!" instead of as the helpful suggestion it was meant to be.

A Holy Man In A Holy Place?

Max's emotions shifted from anger to sadness and pain by the time he sat back down. He looked defeated, as if someone had just punched him in the stomach. I decided to take a risk. I walked up to the whiteboard at the front of the room and wrote:

It's easy to be a holy man in a holy place.

"Max, I can relate to what I think you're feeling," I said. (I won't say, 'I know what you're feeling.' I hate it when people say that to me.) "The first time I, myself, heard the 'stuff' we've been exploring during this meeting, it excited me to the point that I was itching to live the principles. I could not wait to get home and continue the journey with my wife and family. I felt freer than I had ever felt before; people in my group seemed to understand me, which caused me to take some serious risks. I began to connect the dots in my own life; things made so much sense and I felt so good."

Max gave me a tentative smile, which I interpreted to mean that he was open to hearing my experience. "I felt like I think you were feeling earlier on in this workshop. When I left my session, I was filled with the hope and expectation that my good feelings would just build and mature when I got home. In my head I had made up the story that my wife would pick me up at the airport and that she would immediately understand my new and improved self and respond to my deep sharing just as we did here with you and others in our meeting."

Max's emotions seemed to continue to soften, "It was easy for me to feel holy in a holy place, to feel protected in the protected environment of the session I attended. It wasn't long, however, before I had to admit that I was not prepared for the real world yet. Just like you, I threw the baby out with the bath water. Instead of digging deep inside for the feelings I was experiencing and refusing to let anyone throw me off course, I went back to my default switch of the victim who was not appreciated and understood. I went back to my self-protective mantra I had at the time (you may recall my "manifesto" in Chapter 8: "You **gotta** love this kid")."

"I kept thinking, 'What's wrong with the world and the people who *say* they care for me?' I made up the story in my head, 'If my wife really loved me, she'd understand.'" My wife could not instantly understand all that it took me time and work to just begin to understand myself, but I expected she could, just as Max expected my associate to fully understand the impact her feedback would have on him.

"I'm not saying anything is wrong with you, Max. Just like I'm not saying something was wrong with me in that instance, but I am suggesting that you and I can do better **if** we connect the dots and take control of our lives."

"Can I ask you a question?" I was asking for his permission to give him feedback. It was an unenthusiastic reply, but he gave me an affirmative nod. "What were you feeling and how did the feedback impact you?"

"I felt angry and hurt (Feelings). I was a kid again (Identity). And I felt that no matter what I did, I would never get...." He stopped mid-sentence as if he was searching for the next words.... "My mother's approval. I felt that I had taken an enormous leap of faith in the open seat. It caught me off guard and I felt ambushed during the break," he said. "I think it was the exact count—the number 'twenty-three'—that felt like the disappointment I always experienced, "You're never good enough. You'll never measure up.""

Max, his peer-partners and I did have a very productive and satisfying conversation as a closing to the workshop, realizing that he fell into an "unintended trap" of equating my associate's comments with his mother's criticism. Before he left, he attempted to apologize to my associate and admitted that he had hoped to gain her approval during the training event. "I like you and had hoped you liked me," he told her. At the same time, my associate respectfully refused to allow Max to take any blame. She felt that it was her responsibility to apologize for her perceived insensitivity, thereby building mutual trust and understanding.

I'm not going to end this with "And they lived happily ever after." I've since heard from Max that he uses the "unintended trap" as a reminder when he faced similar disappointments later. This type of recycling of memories is not unusual. Don't give up when you begin to apply some of the change initiatives I've been sharing throughout the book. Change is often a slow, repetitive process with missteps along the way.

Remember, it's easy to be a holy man in a holy place.

It's everywhere else that offers us the opportunities to grow as human beings.

CHAPTER 17

"That's Life!"

Living the Life

When and where I grew up — during the 1940s and 1950s in upstate New York — men and women lived their lives floating between memories and anticipation...the past and the future. People did not talk about taking charge of their lives. They simply learned how to adapt and adjust to situations as they arose.

"The past is gone," I was told. "And the future is nothing more than a dream." I initially assumed that this was how things were meant to be since no one seemed upset or was especially curious about anything beyond how things were supposed to play out in life. There was a simple response if someone stuck his head above the normal mindset of acceptance. The street wisdom was as the Frank Sinatra song title says — "That's Life!"

The time-paradox—floating between memories (yesterday) and anticipation (tomorrow)—was more than an intellectual curiosity for me in my younger years. It was a silent void between a past that did not seem fair and a future that was too predictable. Those who dared to dream did so by planning for a loving marriage and stable job.

Occasionally, the bar was raised from a traditional occupation in the footsteps of a family member to an actual independent career. Successful men might build a bigger home and wear a shirt with a white collar instead of the blue collar hanging in their father's closet.

Except for a few extraordinary exceptions or "outliers,[14]" women stayed at home or worked closer to home and did what society encouraged them to do — support and nurture their families. Most couples ended up sitting on the same couch as their parents with a TV remote control pointed towards the only predictable excitement that they could count on — life in a box with a handful of channels.[15]

Be Here Now

I imagined life to be like a hero sandwich. *Now* is the real meat of existence, stuffed between the sweet memories and bitter regrets of the past and the

---

14   "Outliers: The Story of Success" written by Malcolm Gladwell examines the factors that contribute to unusual levels of success in terms of intelligence, expertise and skill, including as it relates to competitiveness and wealth.

15   I trust that you will not read any sarcasm or judgment into my description here. I've been known to struggle for couch control! In fact, I continue to attempt to convince my wife that TV remotes are dangerous and could cause fires if they get in the wrong hands!

hopes and dreams for the future. Therefore, if I wanted to better manage my life, I decided that I had to learn to live in the moment...in the *now*.

I was greatly encouraged when I traveled west in the 1960s in search of a richer consciousness. The truth is I was not just pursuing opportunities to grow. I was also escaping from what felt like a fitting for a straight jacket. I was trapped in a series of conflicts because I was beginning to stray outside of family expectations. I found my way to Esalen, something of a Garden of Eden tucked along the Big Sur coastline of California. I had read that Esalen was a place where people come to explore "the unexplored frontiers of human potential yet to be realized." The article went on to say, "Esalen is a place, as Thomas Wolfe said about America, where miracles not only happen, but where they happen all the time." I was not sure what I would find there, or if I would come away with a feeling of "Baloney" (disappointment) or "wow" (amazement), but I was certainly looking for a miracle.

At Esalen, I was told by an Eastern mystic that if I wanted to truly live life I should "Be Here Now." That was not the first time I had heard that message. I had read it in *Time Magazine* and saw it on TV on Channel 13. But to hear it directly from an Indian shaman was especially powerful. Up to this point I had mistakenly believed that the message was just a hippie conspiracy to drop out of society.

In an effort to Be Here Now, each morning before beginning my day, I would sit perfectly still and stare off into space. But no matter how hard I tried, however, I never quite experienced *now*. The moment kept moving. I gradually began to understand that in this life, nothing is static. There is perpetual energy in everything that surrounds us and time continues to march onward with or without us being consciously involved in the process. You and I are constantly changing, even if we sit on our butts and hold our breath.

The question that kept showing up in my mind was:

How can I take charge of my life?

Later, but still in the 60s, (but this time not in the 1960s, but in my 60s, my age) I'm in the 68th year of my potential 100-year window. My life-journey has rapidly moved on, occasionally without me. I've enjoyed the victories and celebrated the blessed events along the way. I have pictures both on my bookshelf and in my heart as living proof. I've come to realize that I have occasionally missed important parts of my life and from time to time been untrue to my mission to live a mindful[16] life. For example, my thirties and forties are a bit of a blur. I was working so much and was trying so hard to fit into rapidly shifting roles and responsibilities that the years flew by like an extended business lunch meeting.

I don't mean to suggest that I have no recollection of those specific years of my life. I can describe the colored ties I wore. I especially remember the wonderful people I met as a psychologist and executive coach. They have been my best teachers. I recall their stories and learned from both their victories and defeats. I also have some scars and not so heroic memories of my own, of which I've attempted to use as life-lessons to become a better man.

I will admit, I've also had a few humility lessons as a result of occasional thoughtless "DUM" moments. (See Chapter 10 — I <u>D</u>on't <u>U</u>nderstand the <u>M</u>eaning.) If I could not find meaning or lessons learned from them, I mumbled the words, "Oh, well," and buried them in the backyard of my mind.

I consider myself especially lucky to have walked the earth with some very special people who have lightened my load by blessing me when they could have rightfully judged me. All of them have inspired me by raising the bar on what it means to live authentically.

"Connecting the Dots" between the influences of people and events upon an individual's subsequent mindset, attitudes and behaviors has become a major part of my professional work and an even greater part of my personal life. In this final chapter, I attempt to remain focused on the goal of taking this information from a conceptual point of view to a practical methodology for those who wish to become more mindful of their own life journeys. I did my best to honor the balance between talking too much about my life versus not being honest and open. I don't believe that I can expect you to take risks if I don't.

Ten Recommended Steps

I offer you ten recommended steps to help you on your way.

Begin by Looking for Your "Past Future."

I recently headed west again to take another bite out of the "Be Here Now" sandwich that I referred to earlier in this chapter. I spent three days with Sam Keen, an eighty-plus-year-old philosopher with the wit of Woody Allen

---

16 Mindful is a word to describe attempts to "stop and smell the roses" throughout one's life journey. Mindfulness is a key part of the Be Here Now process of celebrating the moments of life.

Dr. Joe Currier

and the soul of an Aristotle. Dr. Keen asked a small group of us mindful life-travelers to review and "re-vision" their life, myself included.

Dr. Keen's overriding question was, "What's next?" He repeated the inquiry in relation to the fact that every decade of the life-cycle brings new challenges, goals, pleasures, and horizons. He reminded us that every major change and transition—birth, marriage, divorce, relocation, death, promotion, demotion, etc.—requires us to make a new beginning, take stock of our past, and look for a new vision to guide us toward a more hopeful future. I was doing what I also encourage you to do after reading these pages. I re-viewed my life with questions like: "How can I continue to 'Connect the Dots' to improve my journey and live more authentically?" "How's it working at this point in my life?" "What's at Risk if I change vs. choosing not to change...."

As I said, Dr. Keen spoke of the "Past Future." He said, "What happened back then will show up at a later date in your life. You cannot move forward on a truly autobiographical life-journey until you identify the myths from the past (false beliefs, self-defeating theories, misperceptions, and assumptions not grounded in reality)."

Buddhist Monks have a collateral perspective to "connect the dots" in our "past future." Interestingly, they ask, "Who were you before everyone wrote on you?" People whom you perceive to be authorities and nurturers shape your future. You begin to live out a life-story before you are even aware of it. I'm hoping that this book will help you to proceed with your eyes wide open and your mind uncluttered by the "stuff" other people "write on you". It's all about choices.

That's what this book is all about. From the sacred wisdom of Buddhist Monks, to a philosopher with a "keen" point of view (pun respectfully intended), to a 68-year-old psychologist, MAP-ing the final chapters of his life, the message is the same. To use a term from the '60s, it's time to "get real." Each of us has an opportunity to better shape our Past Future (current moments that will show up as tomorrow's memories) by first attending to our Past Future (lessons learned from life's marker events). Your POWER (Passion-Ownership-Wellness-Excellence-Relationships as described in Chapter 4.) multiplies when you create your own authentic journey, which, as I've stated so often in a variety of ways, may not be as easy as you suppose. Most of us stumble into each new chapter of our lives, like a teenager on a first date.

People begin to "write on us" and label us before we are even aware of it. Virtues and vices are typically attributed to different members of a family. In early life, we may not even be aware that we have choices. In fact, as children, we come to believe what we believe because that is how we got attention, protection, affiliation, and affection.

In my family, for example, my older brother was the "designated hitter." Jim had a passion to play ball. The only thing that surpassed his outstanding athleticism and love of the game, was the family folklore. Everyone agreed, "Jimmy was playing catch with his father before he could walk." If I were to MAP my brother's life, I could not help but wonder if he kept an intimate connection alive with his first coach, my deceased dad, by performing up to the expectations of future surrogate fathers, men who were there for him during his challenges on and off the field. Early on, he had been "written on" as a top player, and saw no other choices but to remain that.

As I've applied the strategies in this book to the seasons of my life, I have come to wonder about my athletic potential. I played varsity sports, but never pushed myself. Was I afraid that I could not measure up to my older brother (who, by the way, was eventually inducted into the New York State Sports Hall of Fame)? Or was I just seeking my own unique identity in other areas of life? These were some of the great questions that I explored in the early chapters of my life story.

What have people "written on you"? Who would you be (that is to say, how would you think, feel, and behave differently) if no one told you "who you are"? In an effort to explore these and other questions, I invite you to draw your lifeline.

Step 1. Lifeline Exercise

In this exercise, let's look at how marker events impacted you. Using the "My Lifeline" model (Figure 13), draw the peaks (positive events) and valleys (low points) of your life. Go back in time as far as you can go (or choose to go) and label the earliest significant memory as "A," the next earliest marker memory as "B", etc. Choose between as few as five and no more than ten significant life-events.

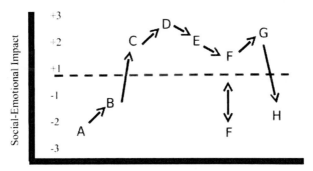

Figure 13.

Place each letter according to the highs and lows of your life. In my example, the "A" and "B" on this simplified version of my lifeline are the "lowest of lows" (-3). The letter "A" represents the events related to the death of my father. "B" represents the decision to separate my brothers and me; we lived apart for a period of time while my mother recovered from the shock and disruption of my dad's fatal car accident. The letter "C" is a proud moment when I was chosen to play on the Little League All Star team. It was the first time my mother and a dear uncle that I looked up came to watch me compete. The letters "D" and "E," highest of highs, are my marriage and the births of my children.

Combining the two letter "Fs" into one dual-impact-event is an example of how a single event can have both positive and negative outcomes. In this instance, I experienced a very confusing and troubling leadership meltdown. The positive impact resulted from the support I received from a man who modeled how real leaders handle tough situations without crossing the line from "passion to abuse." A lifelong friendship resulted that eventually caused me to prosper because of the lessons learned despite the initial trauma to my ego. Another example of a "dual-impact" event (not noted on this chart) would be the effect that cancer had on a former client's life. She said that the life-threatening, painfully traumatic disease/treatment ultimately changed her life for the better. After she survived the cancer, she experienced life from a more mindful perspective, savoring every precious moment.

The letter "G" represents the birth of my grandchildren, while the letter "H" notes the impact of the death of my mother. Marker events can range from simple, yet impacting memories, like winning a spelling bee in eighth grade, to the calamity and sorrow related to death and dying memory moments.

It will help if you continue to explore your lifeline and the lifeline of people very close to you. Life is a never-ending story until the final movie credits roll. The more you truly understand about the continuing key events in life and the impact people who shared the events have had both positively and negatively on you, the better you will be able to "connect the dots" and remain mindful and in control of what motivates and shapes your mindset and subsequent behaviors (Motivation And Perceptions).

Step 2. Lessons Learned

Now that you have selected a number of marker events, the next step is to explore the underlying belief systems that evolved as a result of these life experiences. How did marker event memories mold your past future? This is where you need to add a second part to your lifeline exercise — lessons learned.

On the lines below, next to each letter (corresponding to the events chosen in Step 1, of course), write a word or phrase to describe the positive and/or negative impact each marker event had on you.

A. _____   E. _____

B. _____   F. _____

C. _____   G. _____

D. _____   H. _____

Examine the highs and lows of your life in relation to the beliefs, assumptions, mindsets, and myths that resulted from the negative and/or positive impact you noted. How were you changed by the event? What did you learn in relation to things like optimism vs. pessimism, trust, or loyalty? Did the impact affect your confidence, self-esteem, and worldview? Can you identify any negative, self-defeating beliefs ("bad theories" or false assumptions) that were associated with the event?

Once again, let me demonstrate by using myself as an example. As a result of the isolation I experienced and the silence around the death of my father (as you may recall my recounting in an earlier chapter, after the funeral, no one ever spoke about him; it was as if he just disappeared), I followed the self-defeating theory that it was not okay to speak about troubling events. I also never saw a man cry and was told not to be a baby whenever I felt pain, sadness, and deep disappointment. Therefore, I falsely assumed that "real men don't cry." I was emotionally dishonest during the first half of my life. I never said "ouch" and never asked for help. My distorted belief was that showing pain and sadness was a sign of weakness and that asking for help was like begging.

It is nearly impossible to live authentically and to fully align your physical, mental, and spiritual lives until you unlock, and get right with, the myths and false assumptions from your past that shape your current behavior. Cognitive distortions will redirect you down the wrong paths in life. Secrets will also usurp your power and freedom to take necessary risks to accomplish your mission in life.

The good news is that secrets that are steeped in shame and fear of being judged by people that you value or "need," lose their power when they are no longer secrets. Identifying marker events (Step 1) and recognizing how those events impacted you (Step 2) are essential to making true-life choices, and living authentically.

Step 3. Do NOT Begin With A Plan.

Yes, you read that heading correctly. I suggested that you do *not* begin the next adventure in your life by rushing out and creating a plan. I cannot cite the source of this advice, but I have come to appreciate the idea, "If you don't have a plan, it's one less thing that can go wrong!"

To begin the process of change, you don't need a fixed strategy or plan. You need *dreams*! And where is the best place to look for dreams? Childhood! Wake up the Peter Pan inside of you and fly back to your past future. Who would you be if no one told you who you were when you were younger, before someone "wrote on you"?

In what broad areas of life are you seeking newness? What life-legacy do you hope to leave? Remember WAR? What's-At-Risk if you change? What's-At-Risk if you don't change? If you can't come up with your dreams and you feel blocked, I recommend that you consider your mindset—your "can-do" vs. "can't do" thinking. Did anyone write on you and thus promote either of these beliefs? Dreaming may be outside of your experience, which means that you have not fully explored options and examined the possible routes to a more fulfilling life. But it's important to dream *big*!

Taboo Societal Barriers

I encourage you to look around and model the attitudes and behaviors of individuals who break what I call "taboo" barriers. These are essentially societal limits. Let me explain. When I was a long-distance runner in middle school, my track coach — a world class runner in his younger years — told us that no one could ever run a sub-four-minute mile. He said, "Someone will eventually break Babe Ruth's record of sixty home runs in one season. But the sub-four-minute mile is out of reach. It's an impossibility."

At the time, in the early 1950s, it was a standard and accepted belief that a four minute mile was a physical barrier that no runner could break without causing significant damage to his or her health. The achievement of a sub-four minute mile seemed beyond human possibility, like climbing Mount Everest or walking on the moon once were as well.

As it turns out, I suppose, everyone forgot to tell Roger Bannister that breaking the four-minute mile was impossible. It was a windy spring day in England—May 6, 1954—when Roger Bannister in a meet at Oxford, competing for the British Amateur Athletic Association, ran a mile in 3 minutes, 59.4 seconds.

The unbreakable record had been broken. At age 25, Roger Bannister had made history. He also broke through the four-minute-mile *psychological* barrier, the taboo barrier I mentioned. Fact is, less than a month later, Australian John Landy, a great runner of the day, who had never run faster than within 1.5 seconds of the four-minute barrier, broke Roger Bannister's new record! John Landy ran a mile in 3 minutes and 57.9 seconds in Finland. Soon, many other highly trained, gifted runners followed, breaking through the four-minute-mile physical barrier. Realizing the impossible was indeed possible, they broke through the psychological barrier that otherwise had been embedded in their belief systems.

Our Own Taboo Barriers

Myths —stories invented in order to explain how things work and to make sense out of how events impact us — from family members and other authorities can block your path. There is always a reason when your passion is blocked. When the hero in your story (you) is trapped, or your life-mission is aborted, you are allowing someone else to be involved in the conflict.

Your psyche is often in a tug-of-war between authenticity and the needs for safety, acceptance, recognition, and comfort. I encourage you to explore Maslow's Hierarchy of Needs (Figure 3 in Chapter 6). What level(s) do you tend to operate on? Do you generally feel insecure and make up "necessary lies" to explain your life, like "I'm constantly nervous *because* I do not have enough money in the bank?" Is that truly the *cause*? When the monetary goal is achieved, does the insecurity reappear in a different form? Do you then rationalize the insecurity as a result of not achieving the promotion that you need in order to *feel* like a success, like you are a respected member of an executive team?

Necessary lies keep us on an emotional treadmill. We imagine that the tension will go away as soon as we get something we "need". Necessary lies are like carrots dangled in front of a donkey to keep the animal moving in the same circle. Instead of "connecting the dots" to marker-memory sources that negatively impact the way we think and behave, we typically look for logical, external, safe solutions to our inner tension. The secret behind "necessary lies" is that the resolution to the tension is inside of the *self* and/or an interpersonal effort to achieve acceptance, affection, approval, and affiliation.

Are you competitive and entrepreneurial (page 42, Maslow's Social Level III and Psychological Level IV) because it satisfies a drive toward the self-actualized goal to "be all that you can be"? Or, is it a way to prove to someone that you are a "somebody" ? Is there a need to please someone else at your own expense? At the risk of sounding like a message on a bumper sticker, as mentioned in an earlier chapter, there is a major difference between *being* successful and *feeling* successful.

At one time or another, most of us have gotten stuck in the past, left struggling with our overly sensitive or damaged egos that are the result of negative marker events. In those instances, no matter how competent and able we are, we tend to operate out of self-limiting beliefs— our own taboo barriers — rather than out of actual measures of competency. Also, the polar opposite of this negative self-talk type of behavior is a self-defeating drive for perfection, which is often actually a "CYA"[17] diversion. Don't be slowed down by "could'a—would'a—should'a" excuses. Wealth, material goods, rank, power, and control only provide temporary illusions of safety and well-being. What world record is waiting for you to break?

Step 4. Keep Your "I" Open on Your Life Journey

We are often given the wrong dream! People, even those who love us and wish us happiness and success, may push us in the wrong directions. They may do this not necessarily to hurt or control us, but to move us toward what they may desire or believe would be a rewarding goal, so why not pass it forward?!

It is especially important to know as much as you can about your parents' marker events. There is both DNA and life-events lineage that will automatically shape your belief systems, especially during the period when you are small...when you look up to them and trust whatever they say and do to be the "gospel truth" (which it may be their intention).

---

17   "CYA"... Cover Your Ass...Protect your *self*.

Let me use a hypothetical add-on to the story of Max (see Chapter 16) to illustrate my point. Max's mother survived because of a zero error tolerance. Being right (in her opinion) gave her an identity and the illusion of security and self-worth. His mom also avoided emotional intimacy and the risk of being hurt by maneuvering "content-level" relationships. She pushed Max to get perfect grades so that he could "guarantee his future." An additional hidden agenda behind her constant criticism may be that it also offered her a CYA, ego-protective motivation — a perfect son would signal a perfect mother.

Max's mom's plan for her son was simple. After graduating with a near perfect GPA, Max would go on to law school and eventually establish a lucrative future that he could control. The problem was this was *her* plan for Max, not Max's plan for himself. His mom forgot to ask Max about *his* dreams. She pushed her son, rather than inviting him into her well-intended dreams.

Pursuing what turns out to be the wrong dreams can be of value, particularly when you modify it along the way. This was true in my own life, in fact. When I look back over my past future, I was close to following the right dreams, and people who supported me in my first crack at a vocational dream were helpful, but, I needed to make some serious modifications to my initial career goal. When I was young, I thought I had a calling to the priesthood. In fact, I went into the seminary after graduating from high school.

It was not an easy decision. My girlfriend at the time was very confused by this, as was I actually. When I connect the dots and MAP my coming-of-age behavior, it makes sense however. As I mentioned in my Manifesto (See Chapter 8), my father was killed in a car accident when I was four years old. In my young, impressionable mind, the only heroic male figures in my life at the time were the Lone Ranger, Tonto, and the parish priest. I did not have a horse and never could figure out if "Kemosabe" really meant "friend," so I looked elsewhere.

Not to joke about this, the fact is a strong, consistent male figure in my life and in the community as a whole was our parish priest, who also was the principal of the local school. Father Clement Handron, a newly ordained priest who had studied in Rome, was eager to save souls, and I was in the on-deck-circle waiting for my turn at bat. Put away the shameful priest horror stories in today's news; this was not the case here. Fr. Handron was a truly special man, who may have kept me out of jail. Many of the men in my neighborhood, bless them, had just returned from World War II and struggled to adjust to life without bullets and bombs. Others were packing their bags for Korea. My two maternal uncles were wonderful men, but when they returned from the military, they struggled to make a living and focus on their own families.

Without other male influence, a summer evening ritual got my attention. In that pre-air-conditioning time, our neighbors would sit on the stoops to escape the apartment heat, and Father Handron would stroll by and spend time checking on his flock. Everyone in the community looked up to him. So, I was especially surprised when he called my mother and asked to take me to a local restaurant for dinner. For one thing, it was big deal to go out for a meal in those days. For another thing, I was surprised he would want to invite me anywhere. Did I mention that in Father Handron's first year as school principal, he expelled me and my band of mischievous cohorts? He also threatened to kick our butts if we ever did what we did again! (Don't ask what we did. By today's standards, it was mild and mostly what you might call a case of "kids will be kids"!) In short, I figured Father Handron had written me off as a lost cause.

What began with one dinner became valued mentoring. Wednesday night dinners at Lombardo's with Father H, though rare, became valued treats. Father Handron mentored me with insights about life and discussions regarding my future. What impressed me most was that he listened to me. He never suggested the priesthood or steered me in any particular direction. In fact, he seemed genuinely surprised when I brought it up to him for the first time when I was a senior in high school. I only later found out, that with my mother and a few others in my family, this was *their* dream come true for me! Little did I realize that my past was writing my future in the moment (past future). In the context of the recurring theme of this book, the next chapter of my life was sneaking up on me.

I had not realized how important my becoming a priest was to my mother and a few others in my family until much later when I injured my back and left the seminary on a temporary leave of absence. During the convalescence I had the option to date women. Seminary rules actually encouraged dating in the hopes that it would help clarify the commitment to live a celibate life if a man continued down the path towards ordination. I faced very difficult periods of conflict within the family whenever I moved away from the life of a seminarian. It was then, by happenstance, I met my future wife. Our initially innocent encounter first whispered, and later shouted, in my ear: "Put away the clerical collar and holy water, Father Joe. You're moving on!"

I did not read the signals clearly at the time, mainly because of the family code of silence around conflict, but my mother very much wanted me to be a priest, but did not tell me that she felt that if I left the priesthood I would be making a mistake in her eyes. My mother justified her behavior with explanations that were not based in fact; I could not have a rational discussion because there was none to be found.

A meme[18] planted itself first in my mother and gradually reproduced itself in anyone near her who did not have psychological antibodies to form judgments on their own. The emotional virus spread throughout members of my family. Just like medical viruses, the meme was not visible to the naked eye. My mother never said, "I want you to be a priest." She never told me directly what to do regarding my vocation in life; she was not a selfish woman and she certainly loved my brothers and me. The meme virus is much more subtle. The tension kept rising to a boiling point. I spent many nights huddled in my 1956 DeSoto parked in the back lot of the airport trying to figure out what direction to take.

Also, although Bob Dylan had not sung it yet, as his song so rightly put it, "The times, they were changing!" Uncle Sam was inviting young men (my age!) to take him up on free travel opportunities to Southeast Asia. I needed a vacation from my problems and I had to find a means of support, so I decided not to wait for a draft notice. I joined the United States Marine Corps. After all, they were looking for a few good men, and I considered myself a good guy, even though some at home would dispute that point.

I realized that I lacked a clear identity and needed someone to believe in me and I in them. Semper Fi was enough for me ... after all I had considered myself "always faithful." As much as I hated to leave, I could no longer be what somebody else wanted me to be. My family's love felt conditional. I knew that I had to write my own life story. It was worth the risk. On a steel gray, dank morning, I said goodbye to my dear future wife (my girlfriend at the time) and boarded a plane for boot camp. I had never even flown before, so this was a real adventure.

Will the True Self Please Stand Up?

I'll save you a long story and a box of tissues. I grew up fast and, with the coaching, support and encouragement of some very special people, gradually began to accept the fact that the Marine Corps was a deep source of pride, but not my final career stop.

I had originally thought that I would make the military my career or eventually transfer to the FBI. When I left the Marine base at Quantico, Virginia, for the last time I did not know where my life was taking me; I just knew that another chapter was beginning to write itself.

---

18   As defined earlier, a meme is an attitude, thought, or belief in the mind that can spread to and from other people's minds. For more information, see Glossary of Terms and Text References at back.

As part of a "What's Next" curiosity, I attempted to identify some basic traits that kept showing up in my past future. When I searched my memories and emotions, I kept connecting to strong traits around empathy and compassion for people. From a very early age, I was "Uncle Joe" to the kids in the neighborhood: "Got a problem? Go see Uncle Joe." I had parlayed these natural attributes into a clerical vocation. I was always a concerned and empathetic listener; heck, I was hearing confessions before I tried on a clerical collar.

Being a priest (seminarian) felt good, but something that Father Handron had told me kept troubling me. He cautioned me that being a priest was an incredible calling. However, it is a lonely life. All my life up until then I had lived in the shadow of loneliness. I always dreamt of having a family around me.

As a psychologist I could hear a person's confession, yet dance with my beautiful girlfriend, marry, *and* have a family. That would be *my* dream!

So I invite you: Why not design your life's mission? What dreams did you leave back in the early parts of your life? Again, who were you before people began to write on you?

As you assess and "re-vision" your life, think about new directions. Also consider two other things:

1. What personality traits can you identify and align with
   the roles and responsibility that you are pursuing?

2. Who will you be taking along with you into your dream(s)? I
   recommend that you help pack their bags through deep discussions on all three levels: Content, Emotions, Identity.

Step 5. Important Questions

When you look in the mirror at your self, do you see Ernest Hemingway or Al Roker? Put another way, what I mean is, when it comes to your life—past, present and future—are you an author or weather reporter? Do you create and shape the story line? Like "Papa" Hemingway, do you choose to write exciting, rewarding life-scripts for our hero (that's you!)? Do you create new, fresh adventures? Or, do you simply report, recount, delineate, narrate, detail, explain, rationalize, review, and critique life events...like Al Roker or others, reporting the weather? Call it what you will ... anything other than taking charge of your life may create missed opportunities. When you act as an author to your life, you choose to live authentically (See Chapter 8).

When you merely report how life's winds blow, you run the risk of choosing to suffer. As author, you connect the dots in your life and forge new pathways based on lessons learned from the past. You look back over your lifeline in order to avoid repeating mistakes of self and others. You model the thoughts and actions of heroes who have blessed you, and bless those "teachers" who meant well, but left destructive messages or pushed you instead of invited you along on their life journey.

To author your life means that you say "Yes" *and* "No". **Yes,** you are responsible for the choices you make. You are mindful to surround yourself with well-intentioned individuals who interact with integrity and foster 'win-win' scenarios in good times and in bad. **No,** you are refusing to allow toxic individuals to rain on your parade with their abusive comments and self-serving, destructive behaviors.

There is no room for pessimism, negativity, or hatred in your life. There is ample room for forgiveness. You might remind yourself that people generally do the best that they can; it is your responsibility **not** to get caught up in their "stuff."

Step 6. Find Partners and Build a F.R.E.

Earlier I mentioned an important piece of advice I received many years ago at Esalen from Gregory Bateson. He said:

"It takes two or more people to understand one human being."

We need other people, partners in this process. We don't know what we don't know. We do not have eyes in the back of our heads and therefore benefit when someone watches our backs. This is true when we face real physical threats (there is strength in numbers!) as well as when we climb the corporate ladder. We need F.R.E., a Feedback Rich Environment! The "Executive Rule of Diminishing Feedback"[19] states that the amount of constructive feedback diminishes when an individual's "psychological size" increases as a result of job title, power, authority, and natural attributes that cause people to "look up to" them.

Constructive feedback translates into competitive, leadership, and partnership opportunities when team players operate in a feedback-rich-environment. You will greatly advance your personal and professional objectives when you form committed, passionate relationships in the spirit of "straight talk between partners."

Step 7. Be Patient and Forgiving...

---

19 A series of "Executive Rules" (E-Rules) are described in detail in my book, "Managers Must Lead and Leaders Must Manage."

You will mess up. Learn from your mistakes. Apologize when you're wrong. Then move on!

You are ill advised to worry about making mistakes. The most toxic "mistake" you can make is to not make a decision because you are afraid of screwing up. Whenever possible, avoid repeating DUMB mistakes (repeating the same error). However, DUM (see Chapter 10) mistakes (learning from your errors) are great self-development opportunities.

Thoughtful, well-intentioned, authentic actions that are initially "incorrect" tend to either correct themselves or someone in your F.R.E. will show up to help get you back on track.

Be sure to monitor your self-talk, that ever-vigilant voice in your head. Self-esteem, self-confidence, and will-to-change are impacted positively and negatively, depending on whether you **listen and believe** what the inner voice says vs. simply **listen and learn**.

Dump any negative self-talk that calls you "stupid" or a whole host of abusive labels. Change does not favor abusive self-talk and pessimistic "can't do" threats and criticisms. Celebrate your best effort as you passionately pursue your objectives.

Step 8. You Need a MAP

Remember it's about Motivation And Perceptions!

Motivation is forward looking. Perceptions, while also very important, are backward looking because they have powerful roots in the past that influence nearly everything you do in the future (Dr. Keen's "Past Future"). One without the other is like driving blindfolded down a heavily traveled highway. I recommend that you take off the blindfold of myths from the past future, otherwise you may collide with the oncoming traffic of new opportunities. I also encourage you to invite people along on your travels, but don't let them drive! It's your adventure. When people insist that their route is the "only way," remember, you are hearing *their* truth.

There is *their* truth, *your* truth, and *the* truth. Life is not like math and science. There is no ultimate, one-size-fits-all formula to achieve happiness and well-being. What is **right** for one person in a specific moment may not be correct for him in another moment, let alone valuable for someone else at any time. The key is to act in the moment...Be Here Now.

I agree with Plato's advice: "We can easily forgive a child who is afraid of the dark. The real tragedy is when men are afraid of the light."

Step 9. Change is Always SIMPLE, but Never EASY...

Change is **simple** because we typically know what to do in order to create new directions, but **never easy** because as human beings we fall back on old habits, a desire for comfort, and excuses, Excuses, EXCUSES.

Expect doubt, hesitation, and fear at times. Use your inner resources and the support of your life-partners to keep moving toward your dreams. Look for conceptual and emotional strategies to support your efforts to adapt to the required changes, as well as, build an interpersonal network to break the *excuses-barrier* ... be it motivation or skill set.

"Those Who WON'T Are No Better Than Those Who CAN'T"

Former Baltimore Ravens Head Coach Brian Billick had this stark reminder hanging over his desk during the team's difficult drive to cap off the 2000 season with a victory in Super Bowl XXXV. Having had the privilege to work with Coach Billick, it was clear to me that this message did not lack a spirit of support or caring for his partners. It was the opposite: he expected the best from every one of his players and coaches. Brian set performance-standards as a challenge to **both** those who struggled with personal drive and motivation, as well as, those who needed to raise their fundamental skill-sets. After that, he did everything within his power to help individuals to achieve their personal best.

Whether you need a better **MAP**, that is to say, if you lack motivation and confidence in a particular life-work direction ... OR whether you need to develop better skill sets, be it more effective communication skills or task-related-KSA's (knowledge, skills, and abilities), please listen to Coach Billick, a Super Bowl winner, committed husband, devoted father, and doting grandfather:

"Those who WON'T are no better than those who CAN'T!"

The outcome is the same: **They DON'T** ...

- ✓ They **DON'T** avoid self-defeating detours and dead-ends in life.

- ✓ They **DON'T** live up to the ideals and standards of business partnerships, marriage and parenthood.

- ✓ They **DON'T** leave the sports arena, the boardroom, or the dinner table with a personal best!

Step 10. Inoculate Yourself

Build psychological antibodies! Before you head off in life to parts yet unknown, be sure to inoculate yourself against the meme virus. You are both a vulnerable recipient and a carrier of false beliefs that say "STOP" instead of "Proceed with Caution" and that encourage you to "zig" when you might better "zag" in life.

You can build what I refer to as "psychological antibodies" against the belief distortions of meme viruses. It takes personal resolve and on-going feedback from fellow travelers. Don't "go along to get along." Some of the things you will say and do will upset or confuse people who care about you. Be sure to share your message with grace and wisdom, not command and control. Keep an ongoing, open, full dialogue (content-emotion-identity), but you make the final call. After all is said and done, you will have to face the consequences of the calls you make.

Empty the Sack

It's important to explore, appreciate, and better focus the impact of life's memory moments...what psychiatrist Carl Jung referred to as the shadow side of our lives. It is important to honor, but never accept and indulge, the limitations left by the marker events.

There is tremendous energy locked up in the submerged parts of our self; energy that can propel us on our life's journey once it is understood and redirected from excuses to new directions.

In his writing, "A Little Book on the Human Shadow," poet Robert Bly visualizes a young child as a lively ball of perpetual energy that radiates in all directions. But the parents do not like, nor understand, various parts of the kinetic ball. In order to keep the parents' love and protection, the child hides important parts of himself that they do not like in an invisible bag that he drags behind him. "By the time we go to school," Bly writes, "the bag is quite large. Then our teachers have their say: 'Good children don't get angry over such little things.' So we take our anger and put it in the bag." By the age of twenty, he insists, there is only a small volume of our original energy remaining.

Here's the exciting news: the energy is dormant, not dead. It's waiting for you to empty the load, to convert the lessons learned back into pure energy and to leave the rest behind, to let go and move on in life.

This wonderful life itself is a lesson to be learned, an epic story with twists and turns, ups and downs. Your best bet is to remain open to people, places and things that can support, encourage and share your life journey. But, I propose that your hundred-year-window is a self-guided adventure with other mindful travelers who also keep their "I's" open.

HAPPY TRAILS

One Closing Thought

The next time you hit a bump in the road and someone tells you, "That's life!" let them know that Frank Sinatra did a great job singing that song. But when it comes to your life:

It's Never Too Late to Have a
Happy Childhood!!

GLOSSARY OF TERMS

__Authentic Self__ is a term to describe the true "me," including my self-image, core values, fundamental beliefs, goals, and public persona. When an individual puts on his or her best public face to impress others, it does not mean that the person is being inauthentic. When an individual portrays a "fictional" self in public, the aim is to please others and gain acceptance; one acts in accordance with what he thinks others want, rather than who he really is. People who are more aligned with their "authentic selves" are better equipped to live more closely, both in private and in public, to their full potential and act in accordance with the things they truly value. Tension arises when the authentic self is not consistent with the public self.

__At-Risk Achievers__ (see Figure 9, Chapter 9) are good at what they do, but do not reflect the core cultural values of an organization. They are successful contributors to the business fundamentals and work processes, while not demonstrating the espoused values and cultural norms. For example, an "at-risk" office manager runs a very successful operation on the surface—while sales numbers meet or exceed fiscal expectations, he or she (s/he) does not build effective teams. That is to say, workers may be deflated by their manager's abusive management style, lack loyalty and trust, and take any opportunity to depart when better job offers arise. Extreme examples of "at-risk behaviors" are the Enron employees who posted major profits, but did so with underhanded, unethical, and illegal activities. At-risk achievers are a major challenge to senior associates because they create the dilemma of ultimately dismissing an individual who contributes to the economic bottom line. To turn one's back on the lack of integrity and absence of cultural values will undermine team efforts unless firmly managed and ultimately corrected.

__Care-frontation__ is a variation of the word "confrontation". The first part of the word—"care"—is a reminder that no matter how difficult a conflict may be, in a partnership, it is important not to become abusive or in any way cross the line from passion to abuse. To care-front someone means that you are willing to address conflicts in an honest, direct, yet respectful manner. While the desired corrective action is important, it is not the primary point of the intervention. The main message is that someone cares enough to offer developmental feedback intended to help individuals better develop personal or professional attitudes and behaviors. The intention of such feedback is not to criticize or undermine a partner, but instead to share information that might otherwise be left to fester in an individual's "blind window". People are often unaware of the impact they are creating and remain in a "blind window" until someone cares enough to tell them how their actions are perceived, such as when a child tells a parent how a remembered incident affected them.

* *Dis-ease, a play on the word "disease,"* highlights the important role that stress and tension play in both physical and psychological disorders. If there is not a direct causal relationship for a disease itself, the term "dis-ease" is then meant to illustrate the role that stress management can play in the recovery process. For example, when a person is distressed, blood vessels contract, which slows the flow of blood to sensitive areas. When one manages stress, the opposite happens. Blood that is vital to the healing process flows in a way that accelerates the healing process.

* *DUM* mistakes/behavior (I **D**on't **U**nderstand the **M**eaning) refer to actions in which a person is uninformed and "in the dark" as to the circumstances or conditions about which others are aware. For example, what I do or say is "DUM", not "DUMB," when a new member of a team misperceives a cultural norm. Everyone knows something that s/he does not know, e.g., when I was doing a workshop and kept referring to members of the team as "partners." Someone finally corrected my "DUM" mistake by informing me that in this particular organization, the word "partner" was never used to denote the relationships between co-workers. *Partner* was a clear delineation of stock ownership, voting privilege, and seniority NOT to be used by non-voting members of the company. It was DUM, not DUMB, because I had no way of knowing that this term would signal a visceral response from the partners who lauded a sense of ownership versus non-partners who felt like second-class citizens. I appreciated it when someone alerted me to the cultural error.

* **Emotional Intelligence (EQ)** is a term that first appeared in a doctoral dissertation by Wayne Payne ("A Study of Emotions: Developing Emotional Intelligence") and later popularized by John Mayer and Peter Salovey in their work, "What Is Emotional Intelligence." Salovey and Mayer's conception of Emotional Intelligence strives to define EQ (similar to the concept of IQ ... Intellectual Intelligence) within the confines of the standard criteria for a new intelligence. Following their continuing research, their initial definition of EI was revised to: "The ability to perceive emotion, integrate emotion to facilitate thought, understand emotions and to regulate emotions to promote personal growth."

The ability-based model views emotions as useful sources of information that help one to make sense of, and navigate, the social environment. The model proposes that individuals vary in their ability to process information of an emotional nature and in their ability to relate emotional processing to a wider cognition. This ability is seen to manifest itself in certain adaptive behaviors. The model claims that EI includes four types of abilities:

1. Perceiving emotions – the ability to detect and decipher emotions in faces, pictures, voices, and cultural artifacts—including the ability to identify one's own emotions. Perceiving emotions represents a basic aspect of emotional intelligence, as it makes all other processing of emotional information possible.

2. Using emotions – the ability to harness emotions to facilitate various cognitive activities, such as thinking and problem solving. The emotionally intelligent person can capitalize fully upon his or her changing <u>moods</u> in order to best fit the task at hand.

3. Understanding emotions – the ability to comprehend emotion language and to appreciate complicated relationships among emotions. For example, understanding emotions encompasses the ability to be sensitive to slight variations between emotions, and the ability to recognize and describe how emotions evolve over time.

4. Managing emotions – the ability to regulate emotions in both ourselves and in others. Therefore, the emotionally intelligent person can harness emotions, even negative ones, and manage them to achieve intended goals.

Measurement of the Ability Model

The current measure of Mayer and Salovey's model of EQ, the Mayer-Salovey-Caruso Emotional Intelligence Test (MSCEIT) is based on a series of emotion-based problem-solving items. Consistent with the model's claim of EQ as a type of intelligence, the test is modeled on ability-based IQ tests. By testing a person's abilities on each of the four branches of emotional intelligence, it generates scores for each of the branches as well as a total score.

Mixed models

The model introduced by Daniel Goleman (author or "Emotional Intelligence") focuses on EQ as a wide array of competencies and skills that drive leadership performance. Goleman's model outlines four main EQ constructs:

1. Self-awareness – the ability to read one's emotions and recog-

nize their impact while using gut feelings to guide decisions.

2. Self-management – involves controlling one's emotions and impulses and adapting to changing circumstances.

3. Social awareness – the ability to sense, understand, and react to others' emotions while comprehending social networks.

4. Relationship management – the ability to inspire, influence, and develop others while managing conflict.

Emotional competencies are not innate talents, but rather learned capabilities that must be worked on and can be developed to achieve outstanding performance. Goleman posits that individuals are born with a general emotional intelligence that determines their potential for learning emotional competencies

* Impostor Syndrome, sometimes called Fraud Syndrome, is a psychological phenomenon in which people are unable to appreciate their accomplishments. It is not an officially recognized psychological disorder by the American Psychological Association. The term was coined by clinical psychologists Pauline Clance and Suzanne Imes.

Despite external evidence of their competence, those with the syndrome remain convinced that they are frauds and do not deserve the success they have achieved. Proof of success is dismissed as luck, timing, or as a result of deceiving others into thinking they are more intelligent and competent than they believe themselves to be. The impostor syndrome, in which competent people find it impossible to believe in their own competence, can be viewed as complementary to the Dunning–Kruger effect, in which incompetent people find it impossible to believe in their own incompetence.

* *Loyal Underachiever* (see Figure 9, Chapter 9) is the mirror image of an "At-Risk Achiever" (see above). S/he is passionate, dedicated, and reflects the core cultural values, but does not succeed in the job. Loyal underachievers can create a great deal of tension for manager's who, despite teaching, coaching, encouraging, and managing individuals for performance, are left with the question of whether the individuals should remain in their position. At some point in time, effective managers must take *loyal underachievers* out of their jobs if they do not eventually meet agreed upon expectations and contribute to the bottom line.

* *Motivation* is the driving force which help causes us to achieve goals. Motivation is said to be intrinsic or extrinsic. The term is generally used for humans but, theoretically, it can also be used to describe the causes for animal behavior as well. According to various theories, motivation may be rooted in a basic need to minimize physical pain and maximize pleasure, or it may include specific needs such as eating and resting, or a desired object, goal, state of being, ideal, or it may be attributed to less-apparent reasons such as altruism, selfishness, morality, or avoiding mortality. Conceptually, motivation should not be confused with either volition or optimism.

According to Abraham Maslow's theory of the Hierarchy of Needs:

- Human beings have wants and desires that influence their behavior. Only unsatisfied needs influence behavior, satisfied needs do not.

- Since needs are many, they are arranged in order of importance, from the basic to the complex.

- The person advances to the next level of needs only after the lower level need is at least minimally satisfied.

- The further they progress up the hierarchy, the more individuality, humanness and psychological health a person will show.

Levels of Motivation (see Maslow's Hierarchy of Needs: Chapter 7): One of the many interesting things that Maslow noticed while he worked with monkeys early in his career, was that some needs take precedence over others. For example, if you are hungry and thirsty, you will tend to try to take care of the thirst first. After all, you can do without food for weeks, but you can only do without water for a couple of days! Thirst is a "stronger" need than hunger. Likewise, if you are very thirsty, but someone has put a choke hold on you and you can't breath, which is more important? The need to breathe, of course.

Maslow took these ideas and created his now famous **hierarchy of needs**. Beyond the details of air, water, food, and sex, he laid out five broader layers: the physiological needs, the needs for safety and security, the needs for love and belonging, the needs for esteem, and the need to actualize the self, in that order.

1. **Physiological needs**. These include the needs we have for oxygen, water, protein, salt, sugar, calcium, and other minerals and vitamins. They also include the need to maintain a pH balance (getting too acidic or base will kill you) and temperature (98.6 or near to it). Also, there's the needs to be active, to rest, to sleep, to get rid of wastes (CO_2, sweat, urine, and feces), to avoid pain, and to have sex. Maslow believed, and research supports him, that these are in fact individual needs, and that a lack of, say, vitamin C, will lead to a very specific hunger for things which have in the past provided that vitamin C, e.g., orange juice. The

cravings that some pregnant women have, and the way in which babies eat the most foul tasting baby food, support the idea anecdotally.

2. **Safety and security needs.** When the physiological needs are largely taken care of, this second layer of needs comes into play. You will become increasingly interested in finding safe circumstances, stability and protection. You might develop a need for structure, for order, and safe limits. Looking at it negatively, you become concerned, not with needs like hunger and thirst, but with your fears and anxieties. In the ordinary American adult, this set of needs manifest themselves in the form of our urges to have a home in a safe neighborhood, job security and a nest egg, a good retirement plan and a bit of insurance, and so on.

3. **Love and belonging needs.** When physiological needs and safety needs are, by and large, taken care of, a third layer starts to show up. You begin to feel the need for friends, a sweetheart, children, affectionate relationships in general, even a sense of community. Looked at negatively, you become increasing susceptible to loneliness and social anxieties. In our day-to-day life, we exhibit these needs in our desires to marry, have a family, be a part of a community, a member of a church, a brother in the fraternity, a part of a gang or a bowling team. It is also a part of what we look for in a career.

4. **Esteem needs.** Next, we begin to look for self-esteem. Maslow noted two versions of esteem needs, a lower one and a higher one. The lower one is the need for the respect of others, the need for status, fame, glory, recognition, attention, reputation, appreciation, dignity, and even dominance. The higher form involves the need for self-respect, including such feelings as confidence, competence, achievement, mastery, independence, and freedom. Note that this is the "higher" form because, unlike the respect of others, once you have self-respect, it is a lot harder to lose!

The negative version of these needs is low self-esteem and inferiority complexes. Maslow felt that Alfred Adler, the famous psychoanalyst, was really onto something when he proposed that these were at the roots of many, if not most, of our psychological problems. In modern countries, most of us have what we need in regard to our physiological and safety needs. We, more often than not, have quite a bit of love and belonging, too. It's a little respect that often seems so very hard to achieve!

All of the preceding four levels he calls **deficit needs**, or **D-needs**. If you don't have enough of something, i.e., you have a deficit—thus, you feel the need.

Dr. Joe Currier

But if you get all you need, you feel nothing at all! In other words, they cease to be motivating. As the old blues song goes, "You don't miss your water till your well runs dry!"

Self-actualization: The last level is a bit different. Maslow used a variety of terms to refer to this level: He has called it **growth motivation** (in contrast to deficit motivation), **being needs** (or **B-needs**, in contrast to D-needs), and **self-actualization**.

These are needs that do not involve balance or homeostasis. Once engaged, they continue to be felt. In fact, they are likely to become stronger as we "feed" them! They involve the continuous desire to fulfill potentials, to "be all that you can be." They are a matter of becoming the most complete, the fullest, "you"—hence the term, self-actualization.

In keeping with Maslow's theory up to this point, if you want to be truly self-actualizing, you need to have your lower needs taken care of, at least to a considerable extent. This makes sense: If you are hungry, you are scrambling to get food; if you are unsafe, you have to be continuously on guard; if you are isolated and unloved, you have to satisfy that need; if you have a low sense of self-esteem, you have to be defensive or compensate. When lower needs are unmet, you can't fully devote yourself to fulfilling your potentials.

It isn't surprising, then, the world being as difficult as it can be, that only a small percentage of the world's population is truly, predominantly, self-actualizing. Maslow at one point suggested only about two percent! The question becomes, of course, what exactly does Maslow mean by self-actualization. To answer that, we need to look at the kind of people he called self-actualizers. Fortunately, he did this for us, using a qualitative method called **biographical analysis**.

He began by picking out a group of people, some historical figures, some people he knew, whom he felt clearly met the standard of self-actualization. Included in this august group were Abraham Lincoln, Thomas Jefferson, Albert Einstein, Eleanor Roosevelt, Jane Adams, William James, Albert Schweitzer, Benedict Spinoza, and Aldous Huxley, plus 12 unnamed people who were alive at the time Maslow did his research. He then looked at their biographies, writings, the acts and words of those he knew personally, and so on. From these sources, he developed a list of qualities that seemed characteristic of these people, as opposed to the great mass of us.

These people were **reality-centered**, which means they could differentiate what is fake and dishonest from what is real and genuine. They were **problem-centered**, meaning they treated life's difficulties as problems demanding solutions, not as personal troubles to be railed at or surrendered to. And they had a **different perception of means and ends**. They felt that the ends don't necessarily justify the means, that the means could be ends themselves, and that the means—the journey—was often more important than the ends.

The self-actualizers also had a different way of relating to others. First, they enjoyed **solitude**, and were comfortable being alone. And they enjoyed deeper **personal relations** with a few close friends and family members, rather than more shallow relationships with many people. They enjoyed **autonomy**, a relative independence from physical and social needs. And they **resisted enculturation**, that is, they were not susceptible to social pressure to be "well adjusted" or to "fit in"—they were, in fact, nonconformists in the best sense.

Maslow further described them as having an **"unhostile" sense of humor**—preferring to joke at their own expense, or at the human condition, and never directing their humor at others. They had a quality he called **acceptance of self and others**, by which he meant that these people would be more likely to take you as you are than try to change you into what they thought you should be. This same acceptance applied to their attitudes towards themselves. If some quality of theirs wasn't harmful, they let it be, even enjoying it as a personal quirk. On the other hand, they were often strongly motivated to change negative qualities in themselves that could be changed. Along with this comes **spontaneity and simplicity**. They preferred being themselves rather than being pretentious or artificial. In fact, for all their nonconformity, he found that they tended to be conventional on the surface, just where less self-actualizing nonconformists tend to be the most dramatic.

Further, they had a sense of **humility and respect** towards others—something Maslow also called democratic values—meaning that they were open to ethnic and individual variety, even treasuring it. They had a quality Maslow called **human kinship** or *Gemeinschaftsgefühl*—social interest, compassion, humanity. And this was accompanied by a **strong ethics**, which was spiritual but seldom conventionally religious in nature.

* *MAP* is an acronym to describe two key factors that determine our choices and behaviors, viz., **M**otivation **A**nd **P**erception. Motivation is the passion that drives individuals to perform in one way vs. another. Perception is the underlying beliefs that also determine behavior. While perception may not be accurate, it is what causes people to think, feel and behave as they do.

* *Marker Events* are significant life experiences beginning with traditional date related events, e.g., birthday, graduation, and death of a loved one. Marker events are any experience that an individual believes is of importance and has

helped to shape his/her life. Markers events are said to help "make me the person that I am today." They can be positive or negative.

* **Marker Memory** is a recollection of an important event in an individual's personal or professional life. For example, the first time a sales person hits the "contest", marking an above average level of success and causing her to stand out as a major player in a highly competitive organization. Small acts of compassion can become significant marker memories to a person in need, e.g., John (not his real name) attempted to revive his dying relationship with his wife. Despite his best effort, he was devastated when his beloved looked him in the eyes and told him, "I don't love you." He recalls, "It felt like a wave of hopelessness swallowed me," and admitted that he was not sure if he would take his own life. When he returned to work with a look of utter despair on his face, a friend asked him to come into his private office. The memory that he claims he will never forget was when this hulk of a man simply reached out and in his words, "Give me a hug that told me that my life was not over. It felt as if someone truly cared for me." This act of kindness forever cemented a friendship between these two men and marked a new day in his life.

* **Meme** (rhymes with the word 'team') is a unit of social information. It is a term coined by Dr. Richard Dawkins in his book *The Selfish Gene*. Memes are attitudes, thoughts, and beliefs in the mind that spread to and from other people's minds. A meme is the basic building block of culture and a key factor in how individuals communicate. If you liken the human mind to a computer, memes are the software part of your programming. Individuals develop types of default responses based on ideas that we believe are true—thoughts and feelings that form the core of our belief systems. The key question is, are they true for you? Or, are they myths and false, self-defeating beliefs from important individuals from your past and culture in which you were raised?

A woman might have in mind a meme like, "It's good to be aware of the current fashion." An associated meme might tell her, "Women who dress fashionably get ahead in life." A third connected meme might solidify into a belief: "Good women want to get ahead, therefore are always well groomed."

Memes are like cognitive viruses that spread from person to person, making unique connections and embedding themselves as core beliefs. But all memetic truths are actually half-truths ... half related to where they were originally hosted and later connected to an individual's distinct beliefs. Little boys learn quickly that certain emotions are acceptable and others are signs of weakness. Memes in this instance can be transmitted by what a father does and does NOT do ... such as when tragedy strikes and men act like the rock in the family by never shedding a tear. The mythic meme that "real men don't cry" is also spread by the abusive tone of a parent who threatens a child, "I'll give you something to cry about," when the youngster shows fear at being inoculated by a pediatrician.

Harmful, negative thinking can be the result of infectious mind viruses. Once a meme is in our minds, it can and will both consciously and subliminally influence our behavior. This is one way that human beings acquire a huge cache of excuses and alibis that keep us in our behavioral rut. Dr. Richard Brodie emphasizes the viral nature of historic memories and describes what happens in the mind through mimicking, modeling and imitating. He notes that the nature of a virus is to reproduce itself ... to make copies of itself as often as possible and to penetrate all available openings, thus spreading itself to as many hosts as possible.

Dr. Brodie, in his work "*Virus of the Mind*," shows that by the age of six or seven, all of us have been programmed with a massive inventory of memes that act like a virus. Attitudes, thoughts and behaviors are repeated and passed on to others, like a virus spreads from person to person in the cold and flu season.

Special memories die hard because they become who we think we are. Core beliefs (such as, "I'm a pessimist; I've always looked at life through a half-empty perspective") die hard because they are memetically fixed in our minds to the point that they form a part of our identity. These beliefs gradually spread throughout our social milieu and form filters of how people perceive us. It is important to figuratively "inoculate" ourselves against memes in order to think for ourselves, rather than adopt the attitudes and behaviors of others.

* **Mindfulness** plays a central part in the teaching of Buddhist meditation. Described as calm awareness of one's bodily functions, feelings, content of consciousness, or consciousness itself, it is the seventh element of the Noble Eightfold Path, the Buddhist development of wisdom. Mindfulness practice is increasingly employed in Western psychology to alleviate a variety of physical and mental conditions. I use the term to remind individuals of the importance of staying in the moment (Be Here Now) in order to avoid myths and false beliefs from the past, habits that could otherwise negatively influence the choices that we make.

* **Necessary Lies** are excuses offered in order to rationalize negative, self-defeating behaviors. For example, the overly punitive parent who justifies his abusive behavior when a child spills his milk with the rationale, "I'm just trying to help my son to develop good table manners." Or the deeply insecure salesman who tells himself that he will slow down and feel less threatened when he builds a reasonable bank account. However, he coins another excuse to explain his underlying insecurity when he has reached his economic goal. Necessary lies are rational explanations that distract individuals from the

historic fears they face as a result of early trauma. When people connect the dots in their lives, they are better able to identify and avoid this frustrating cycle of excuses.

* **Peak Performance** is a dynamic combination of both a physical and mental state of operation in which a person in an activity is fully immersed in a feeling of energized focus, full involvement, and success in the process of the activity. Mihaly Csikszentmihalyi described the state of peak performance as "flow." According to his research, flow is completely focused motivation. It is a single-minded immersion and represents perhaps the ultimate in harnessing the emotions in the service of performing and learning. In flow, the emotions are not just contained and channeled, but positive, energized, and aligned with the task at hand. The hallmark of peak performance is a feeling of spontaneous joy, even rapture, while performing a task. Colloquial terms for this or similar mental states include: to be *on the ball, in the moment, present, in the zone, wired in, in the groove,* or *keeping your head in the game.*

* **Perception**: In philosophy, psychology, and cognitive science, perception is the process by which organisms interpret and organize sensations to produce a meaningful experience of the world. Douglas Adams, a noted researcher in the field, says, "Everything you see or hear or experience in any way at all is specific to you. You create a universe by perceiving it, so everything in the universe you perceive is specific to you." A variation of the saying, "Perception is reality", predicts that "perception may not be accurate, but it is what causes people to think, feel and respond in a specific manner.

The processes of perception routinely alter what humans see. When people view something with a preconceived concept about it, they tend to take those concepts and see them whether or not they are there. This problem stems from the fact that humans are unable to understand new information, without the inherent bias of their previous knowledge. A person's knowledge creates his or her reality as much as the truth, because the human mind can only con-template that to which it has been exposed. The "P" in the concept of "MAP" that I refer to throughout the book means that your perceptions arise in rela-tion to your multiple life experiences, many of which may have been relevant in an earlier stage, but might need to be reexamined to avoid any self-defeating influences from the past

* **POWER** is an acronym that denotes the combined forces that determine peak performance:

Passion—Ownership—Wellness—Excellence—Relationships.

* **Psychodrama** is a method of psychotherapy in which clients are encouraged to explore their personal and interpersonal conflicts through dramatization

and role-playing. Both verbal and non-verbal communications are utilized. Developed by Dr. Jacob L. Moreno, psychodrama has strong elements of theater, often conducted on a stage where props can be used. The audience is fully involved with the dramatic action.

I use to term **psychodrama** to describe recurring emotional scenarios between individuals who share common bonds within a family or a variety of social and/or business bonds. Recurring scenes are acted out, depicting memories of unresolved conflicts, fantasies, dreams, preparations for future risk-taking situations, or unrehearsed expressions of mental states in the here and now. Children raised in abusive environments will often act out in a similar fashion as an out-of-control parent, modeling the very behavior that traumatized them and left with the unfulfilled promise, "I will never treat my wife and children that way." The concept of a recurring psychodrama is the pattern that repeats itself similar to the soap opera that repeats the same theme over and over. Until a person connects the dots from the past, s/he may continue to repeat the mistakes of the past by adopting the attitudes and behaviors that caused the problems in the first place.

* **Psychological Inoculation** is a metaphor to describe the importance to being able to protect yourself from the "viral" meme cycle. By MAP-ing my behavior—better understanding the **m**otives **a**nd underlying **p**erceptions that determine my choices—I can think for myself, rather than suffer the ill-effects of modeling attitudes and behaviors that belong to other people.

* **Psychological Size** refers to the perception that others can have of people in positions of power, authority, and expertise. As business professionals move up the ladder from individual contributor to manger to director to VP and beyond, they often still think of themselves as just good old John and Mary. They don't realize that others perceive them as having larger *psychological size* because of the power that formal organizational authority and admired per-sonal traits confer on them. Everything they say, everything they do is now larger than life and has great power to influence others for good or bad.

Jennifer Joyce and Patty Beach refer to this perceived status as "the Bruce Springsteen effect." They advise individuals with psychological size to imagine that they are like Bruce Springsteen at a concert— "The noted rock star is up on the 25 foot screen, broadcast at 10 times his actual size—every bead of sweat on his brow and every coin in his jeans eminently visible."

That is what every leader from parents in a family, highly accomplished athletes, ranking officers in the military, to senior associates at work must envision when they open their mouths or make any moves. As the late Mrs. Elizabeth Edwards realized following a television interview, whether or not she is aware of the power of her psychological size, others will expect true leadership behavior and judge her harshly if not demonstrated. As a leader, she was reminded that she is always on the big screen. Mrs. Edwards was on the Today Show with Matt Lauer prior to her death. She was discussing her failed marriage and things that led up to it. Mrs. Edwards said "I thought of the people who worked in the campaign not as people who worked for John or worked for me, but as people with whom I worked. I thought of us as equals... If I argued about a policy, I thought I was arguing as an equal. Clearly they didn't have that perception—they thought I was the boss's wife. I didn't take that into consideration." When the boss is a senator and a presidential candidate being the boss's wife is indeed a position of power.

One of the key reminders for individuals who believe that they can diminish their psychological size by acting like "one of the guys", is that psychological size has more to do with what the other person thinks and feels. The perceptions of the men and women who are impacted by the power, authority, and individual traits that project "size" have more to do with how much "size" a person carries than with the rank and traits themselves or an individual's attempts to lower their size.

* **Psychological Well-Being** is not meant as a formal diagnostic category, but instead an individual's perception of how life is treating him/her. It refers to a balance between the combined forces of self-confidence (a sense of optimism and best effort in relation to what I can and cannot do) and self-esteem (a sense of healthy acceptance for the person I am and hope to become).

* **R-Factor** refers to the level of **R**elationship people share. Three primary levels of relationships are described in Chapter 3.

* **Self-Talk** refers to the ongoing internal conversation with ourselves, which influences how we feel and behave. For example, you find yourself in a traffic jam while rushing to work one morning. Your self-talk could be pessimistic and you might think, "My whole day is ruined. If I don't get to work on time, I'll never hear the end of it. My boss will think that I'm not motivated and will surely pass me up for that promotion I've been working all year for." You will then start your day in a bad mood and feel deflated thinking that there's no point in working hard since you already ruined your chances for a promotion. From an optimistic perspective, you could have a more positive internal dialogue (self-talk) and think, "I'll probably be no more than ten minutes late. I guess I'll just have to take a quick lunch instead of going out to eat. If I can turn in my report before the end of the day and make sure that it's error-free, I might still have a chance to get that raise I've been working for."

Researchers such as Dr. John Izzo estimate that an average human being has approximately 45,000 to 55,000 thoughts per day, a veritable non-stop internal conversation. Most of our thoughts are benign, but many of them have a major impact on how we see ourselves. We undermine the growth and development of a healthy sense of self when we feed ourselves a diet of negative self-talk like, "I am stupid ... I'm such a loser," when we face conflict situations.

TEXT REFERENCES

* Bateson, Gregory (May, 9, 1904 – July 4, 1980). A British anthropologist, Cambridge scholar, social scientist, linguist, anthropologist, and cyberneticist whose work intersected that of many other fields. He is noted for his natural ability to recognize order and pattern in the universe. In the 1940s he helped extend systems theory/ cybernetics to the social/behavioral sciences, and spent the last decade of his life developing a "meta-science" of epistemology to bring together the various early forms of systems theory developing in various fields of science. Some of his most noted writings are to be found in his books, *Steps to an Ecology of Mind* (1972) and *Mind and Nature* (1979). *Angels Fear* (published posthumously in 1987) was co-authored by his daughter (from his first marriage to noted cultural anthropologist Margaret Mead) Mary Catherine Bateson.

* Billick, Brian. Former Super Bowl winning head coach of the Baltimore Ravens who is currently a National Football League game analyst for FOX television. He was previously an NFL head coach with the Baltimore Ravens from January 1999 to December 31, 2007. Coach Billick led the Ravens to a 34-7 victory over the New York Giants in Super Bowl XXXV, the franchises only Super Bowl appearance. He was also notable for being offensive coordinator for the Minnesota Vikings (1992-1998) when he broke the then scoring record in the 1998 season. Coach Billick is the author of a number of books, including *More Than a Game* and *Competitive Leadership: Twelve Principles for Success.*

* Bly, Robert. American poet, author, activist and leader of the Mythopoetic Men's Movement. Much of Bly's writings including, *Iron John: A Book About Men,* focus on what he saw as the troubled situation of men in today's world as a result of, among other things, the decline of the father's role in the modern family. He claimed that whereas women are helped by their own bodies along the stages of maturity, men are somewhat of an "experimental species" and have to be taught what it is to be a man. Older cultures had elaborate myths, enacted through rites of passage, that helped men along this path as well as the concept of a "men's societie" as a place where older men would teach young boys on these gender specific issues. Bly argues that these rituals are as important to humans as instincts are to animals and as fathers became increasingly absent from the house during and after the industrial revolution, young males did not receive the teachings that they used to. According to Bly, many of the phenomena of depression, juvenile delinquency and lack of leadership in business and politics have their roots in these problems.

* Dyer, Wayne Walter. An American self-help advocate, author, and lecturer. Although Dr. Dyer resisted the spiritual tag, by the 1990s he was altering his message to include more components of spirituality, e.g., in his books, *Real Magic* and *Your Sacred Self.* He is widely recognized for his television and speaking engagements. His latest book/CD series are, *Excuses Begone!* and *The Power of Intentions.*

* Fassel, Jim (James Edward Fassel). Head coach and president of the Las Vegas Locomotives of the United Football League. He is widely known as the former head coach of the NFL's New York Giants and Offensive Coordinator of the Baltimore Ravens. Coach Fassel began his career with assistant coaching stints at the University of Utah and Stanford University, working with John Elway at Stanford. He later served as head coach of Utah. Coach Fassel has a long record of offensive success. He tutored prominent quarterbacks Phil Simms and John Elway. Prior to becoming New York Giants head coach, Fassel served as an assistant coach with the Arizona Cardinals, Denver Broncos, New York Giants, and Oakland Raiders. During Fassel's time as Giants head coach, his teams were known for numerous post-season runs and for winning big games, such as against the previously undefeated Denver Broncos in 1998. In 1997, he was named NFL coach of the year.

* Jung, Carl Gustav (26 July 1875 – 6 June 1961). A Swiss psychiatrist, an influential thinker, and the founder of analytical psychology. Jung is often considered the first modern psychologist to state that the human psyche is "by nature religious" and to explore it in depth. Though not the first to analyze dreams, he has become perhaps one of the most well known pioneers in the field of dream analysis. He considered the process of individuation necessary for a person to become whole. This is a psychological process of integrating the opposites including the conscious with the unconscious while still maintaining their relative autonomy. Individuation was the central concept of analytical psychology. Many pioneering psychological concepts were originally proposed by Jung, including the Archetype, the Collective Unconscious, the Complex, and synchronicity. A popular psychometric instrument, the Myers-Briggs Type Indicator (MBTI), has been principally developed from Jung's theories.

* Maslow, Abraham. Psychologist who (see Motivation and Hierarchy of Needs, Chapter 6) began teaching full time at Brooklyn College. During this period of his life, he came into contact with the many European intellectuals that were immigrating to the US, and Brooklyn in particular, at that time—people like Alfred Adler, Erich Fromm, Karen Horney, as well as several Gestalt and Freudian psychologists. Maslow served as the chair of the psychology department at Brandeis from 1951 to 1969. Through his books and teachings he is credited with the Self-Actualization theory, Maslow's hierarchy of needs, and many more concepts that have improved life for humanity as a whole.

BIBLIOGRAPHY

Boyatzis, Richard, Fran Johnston and Annie McKee, *Becoming a Resonant Leader: Develop Your Emotional Intelligence, Renew Your Relationships, Sustain Your Effectiveness.*

Brodie, Richard, *Virus of the Mind: The New Science of the Meme.*

Covey, Stephen Richards, *The Seven Habits of Highly Effective People*

Principle-Centered Leadership

First Things First

Covey, Stephen M.R., Stephen R. Covey and Rebecca R. Merrill, *The Speed of Trust: The One Thing That Changes Everything.*

Currier, Joseph R., *Managers Must Lead and Leaders Must Manage*

10 Leadership Contracts: Key Strategies To Build POWER Teams

Leadership Is Always Simple But Never Easy

If You're So Damn Smart, Why Aren't You Healthier and More Effective?

Audio Collections:

Less Stress

How to Manage Stress

It's a WellinWorld : six story book-audio series for children

Dawkins, Richard, *The Selfish Gene.*

Eisenstat, Russell, Michael Beers, et. al., *How High-Commitment High-Performance (HCHP) Organizations Profit*, Harvard Business Review, July-August 2008.

Gladwell, Malcolm, *Outliers: The Story of Success.*

Goleman, Daniel, *Emotional Intelligence*

Primal Leadership: Realizing the Power of Emotional Intelligence.

Izzo, John, *The Five Secrets You Must Discover Before You Die.*

Keen, Sam, *Fire in the Belly: On Being a Man,* and *Your Mythic Journey: Finding Meaning in Your Life through Writing and Storytelling.*

Lipton, Bruce H. *Unleashing the Power of Consciousness, Matter,* and *Miracles* and *The Wisdom of the Cells: How Your Beliefs Control Your Biology.*

Seligman, Martin, *Learned Optimism.*

Stone, Douglas, Bruce Patton, and Sheila Heen, *"Difficult Conversations: How to Discuss What Matters Most"*

Williamson, Marianne, *"A Return to Love: Reflections on the Principles of 'A Course in Miracles'"*

ABOUT THE AUTHOR

Joseph R. Currier, Ph.D., is a licensed psychologist and management consultant, who has devoted his career to helping people change the self-defeating attitudes and break through barriers of resistance that prevent them from leading healthier, happier, and more productive lives.

In his years of professional dedication, Dr. Currier has been involved in leadership development, executive coaching, succession planning, change-transition management, crisis intervention and team building with a wide variety of organizations such as The Allegis Group, Baltimore Ravens NFL Franchise, Mobil Oil, KPMG, Wachovia Bank and the United States Forest Service. He frequently serves as a personal coach and consultant to senior executives, professional athletes and team coaches.

Dr. Currier is the Chief Learning Officer for The Allegis Group, helping to establish a corporate university and directing its Executive Institute. Joe has been a senior psychological associate with four of the premier outplacement companies: Jannotta Bray, Right Associates, Lee Hecht Harrison and Drake Beam Morin. He is a faculty member of the Bernard H. Ehrlich Executive Management Institute (EMI) at the University of Maryland, and a former professor and graduate department chairperson at Hofstra University.

Dr. Currier is the author of the book-audio series, *"Leadership Is Always Simple But Never Easy."* His innovative work to foster personal and professional growth include workshops like: *"The Art of Leadership"*, *"Lead, Follow, OR Hide,"* and *"Survive OR Prosper."*

Joe also wrote and narrated two other audio series: *"How to Manage Stress"* and *"Less Stress,"* as well as, authored, *"Connect the Dots—How Significant Life Events Impact Your Life, Leadership Style and Competitive Performance,"* *"Managers Must Lead and Leaders Must Manage"*, and *"If You're So Damn Smart, Why Aren't You Healthier and More Effective?"*

To learn more about Dr. Joe Currier and his work with the Currier Consulting Group, Inc., you can contact him at: Joe@currierconsultinggroup.com or visit the website: CurrierConsultingGroup.com

CPSIA information can be obtained
at www.ICGtesting.com
Printed in the USA
FFOW05n1821260914